DANIEL

Also by James Montgomery Boice

DANIEL

An Expositional Commentary

JAMES MONTGOMERY BOICE

BakerBooks
Grand Rapids, Michigan

© 1989 by James Montgomery Boice

Published by Baker Books
a division of Baker Publishing Group
P.O. Box 6287, Grand Rapids, MI 49516-6287
www.bakerbooks.com

Paperback edition published 2006
ISBN 10: 0-8010-6641-7
ISBN 978-0-8010-6641-2

Second printing, September 2007

Previously published by Zondervan

Printed in the United States of America

        The Library of Congress has cataloged the hardcover edition as follows:
Boice, James Montgomery, 1938–
        Daniel : an expositional commentary / James Montgomery Boice.
            p.   cm.
        Originally published: Grand Rapids, MI : Ministry Resources Library, © 1989.
        Includes bibliographical references and index.
        ISBN 10: 0-8010-1258-9 (cloth)
        ISBN 978-0-8010-1258-7 (cloth)
        1. Bible. O.T. Daniel—Commentaries. I. Title
BS1555. 53. B65 2003
224′.5077—dc21   2002154565

To the living God
who endures forever
whose kingdom will not be destroyed
and whose dominion will never end

Contents

Preface

One spring a number of years ago when the Philadelphia Conference on Reformed Theology was meeting in five separate cities, I assigned the subject "God and History" to five different speakers to see what they would do with this theme. Each approached the theme well and in his own way. But I was particularly impressed with one speaker who addressed the subject by a study of the Book of Daniel. His point was that Daniel gives the meaning of history more clearly than any other portion of the Bible and, what is more, it tells us how to live for God in ungodly times—like our own.

Do many people regard Daniel as a clear revelation of the meaning of history—or of anything else for that matter? I doubt it! Yet that is what it is.

Some approach this book as if it were a puzzle given to stretch our minds and put us through our paces as students called to "compare Scripture with Scripture" to figure things out. There is an evangelical version of this that focuses on prophetic portions of the book. It tries to explain the time frame in which Messiah was to come, be cut off, and then come again in glory. There is also a liberal version in which the traditional authorship of Daniel is denied and the chief emphasis is placed on answering questions like: Who wrote Daniel actually? When was it written actually? And why did the writer pretend to be foretelling future events when he was actually only recording history?

No one can doubt that there are puzzling elements to this prophecy. At one point Daniel himself was puzzled, and there are parts of his book that have never (in my opinion) been conclusively explained. But to think of Daniel chiefly as a puzzle is to miss its extraordinary relevance, which is why my friend who spoke at the Philadelphia Conference of Reformed Theology was so eager to examine this book for its illuminating insights into history. Consider these facts:

9

1. Daniel was a godly man sent to live in ungodly Babylon at a time when God's blessing upon the Jewish nation seemed to have been withdrawn or postponed. This means that his position was much like that of believers trying to live in secular society today.

2. The Babylon of Daniel's day was a type of all kingdoms that do not acknowledge God or think they can dispense with him. This is an apt description of most of the world in our time, including so-called "Christian" America.

3. Daniel (and his three friends Hananiah, Mishael, and Azariah) was under tremendous pressure to conform. That is, his religion was tolerated, even respected, as long as he did not allow it to intrude into public life or "rock the ship" of state. That is our situation also. We can practice our religion so long as it is not in the schools, at work, or in any public place. We have to keep it "on the reservation."

4. The world seemed to be winning. Nebuchadnezzar (and after him Belshazzar) reigned. Nebuchadnezzar believed himself to be above having to answer to anybody.

5. Nevertheless, in spite of these things, God told Daniel that it is he, God, who is in control of history and that his purposes are being accomplished, even in the overthrow and captivity of his people. Moreover, in the end God will establish a kingdom that will endure forever. The destiny of the people of God is wrapped up in that eternal kingdom.

I do not know of any message that is so timely and valuable for Christians living in our own secular and materialistic times as that message is. Indeed, in Daniel we have a stirring and helpful example of one who not only lived through such times and survived them but who actually triumphed in them and excelled in public life to the glory of God. Daniel did not compromise. He did not bow to this world's idols. He was hated and plotted against. But he triumphed because he knew God and trusted him to do with his life whatever was best. One of my favorite quotations in all the Bible is from this book, and it makes precisely that point. It is from the scene in which Daniel's friends have been summoned before King Nebuchadnezzar for their refusal to bow before the golden statue and explain why they will not bow down.

O Nebuchadnezzar, we do not need to defend ourselves before you in this matter. If we are thrown into the blazing furnace, the God we serve is able to save us from it, and he will rescue us from your hand, O king. But even if he does not, we want you to know, O king, that we will not serve your gods or worship the image of gold you have set up.

Daniel 3:16–18

We need people like that today—people who are aware of the dangers of trying to serve God in this world but who trust God in spite of the danger and who will not compromise. They are the only ones who really triumph, regardless of appearances, and in the last analysis, they are the ones who make a difference.

This is the only book in the Bible that I have preached through twice for the benefit of my own congregation, once many years ago and a second time more recently. It was even better the second time.

I want to thank the congregation of Tenth Presbyterian Church for letting me do the study necessary for the preparation of such sermons and for the time to write them for the benefit of others. I also want to thank my excellent secretary Caecilie M. Foelster, who types the manuscripts and checks them for accuracy. She has made my work much easier and has greatly increased the volume of work I have been able to accomplish.

I dedicate this volume to the living God, who endures forever, whose kingdom will not be destroyed, and whose dominion will never end (Dan. 6:26).

James Montgomery Boice
Philadelphia, Pennsylvania

1

Whose God Is God?

Daniel 1:1-2

In the third year of the reign of Jehoiakim king of Judah, Nebuchadnezzar king of Babylon came to Jerusalem and besieged it. And the Lord delivered Jehoiakim king of Judah into his hand, along with some of the articles from the temple of God. These he carried off to the temple of his god in Babylonia and put in the treasure house of his god.

Tucked between the great Old Testament prophecies of Isaiah, Jeremiah, and Ezekiel on the one hand, and the twelve minor prophets that conclude the Old Testament on the other, lies Daniel. Jesus called Daniel a prophet, thus validating both the man and his function (Matt. 24:15). But in spite of this authentication, the Book of Daniel has been more vigorously attacked by higher critics of the Old Testament than perhaps any comparable passage of Scripture. One commentator flatly calls it "allegory."[1] Another says that it *"purports* to give the story of one Daniel who suffered the first exile under Nebuchadnezzar and lived in the Eastern Diaspora" but that it was actually written much later, after the events it purports to prophesy had happened.[2]

The nineteenth-century scholar and churchman E. B. Pusey had it right when he wrote, "The book of Daniel is especially fitted to be a battleground between faith and unbelief. It admits of no half-way measures. It is either divine or an imposture."[3]

13

The Importance of Daniel

What is the value of Daniel apart from its having become a battleground between faith and unbelief? The large proportion of the book given to prophecy is one measure of its value—as well as the main reason for its having become a battleground. But it is not the whole basis for the book's place in the canon. True, there is a great deal of prophecy. Daniel predicts the precise year of the appearance of Jesus Christ (cf. Dan. 9:25–26). He foretells the history of his portion of the world from the time of Nebuchadnezzar up to the beginning of the Christian era, accurately forecasting the rise and fall of the Medes and Persians, the Greek kingdom of Alexander the Great and his successors, and Rome. He speaks of some things yet to come. Although these predictions are important, they are not necessarily the most important themes in Daniel.

What is the chief or most important theme? This is not a hard question, nor do we have to go far for an answer. The theme is stated at the very beginning in the words that give a historical setting for the story. "In the third year of the reign of Jehoiakim king of Judah, Nebuchadnezzar king of Babylon came to Jerusalem and besieged it. And the Lord delivered Jehoiakim king of Judah into his hand, along with some of the articles from the temple of God. These he carried off to the temple of his god in Babylonia and put in the treasure house of his god" (Daniel 1:1–2).

By way of historical background it is helpful to know that Nebuchadnezzar attacked the southern Jewish kingdom of Judah three times, beginning in 605 B.C., a little more than a hundred years after the northern kingdom of Israel had fallen to the Assyrians.

The second invasion occurred in 597 B.C., when Jehoiakim, son of the king of Judah mentioned in Daniel 1:1–2, was compelled to surrender Jerusalem and go into captivity with many of the Jewish leaders, including the royal family, the commanders of the army, craftsmen, and even some of the priests like Ezekiel. The third invasion was the one we remember most. It took place in 586 B.C. when Jerusalem was completely destroyed and the people of the land were deported to Babylon. Jeremiah was in Jerusalem at the time of this final destruction of the city.

Since Daniel begins by relating the events of the book to the deliverance of King Jehoiakim into Nebuchadnezzar's hands, it must have been through the first of these three invasions that Daniel and his friends Hananiah (renamed Shadrach), Mishael (Meshach), and Azariah (Abednego) were taken from Jerusalem to Babylon to be trained for Nebuchadnezzar's service.

The interesting thing about his beginning of the book, however, is that it is not the four men, whose stories will be told in subsequent chapters, who are said to have been brought back to Babylon by Nebuchadnezzar but rather "the articles from the temple of God" that Nebuchadnezzar "put in the treasure house of his god." That is no incidental or irrelevant beginning. On the contrary, it is the theme of the book and the key to everything that follows.

As the story will show, Nebuchadnezzar was an exceedingly arrogant man, and the conquests he made were understood by him to be proof of his superiority (or the superiority of his gods, which he did not always clearly distinguish from himself) to all others. Jews boasted that their God, Jehovah, was all-powerful. Nebuchadnezzar believed that he was greater than that God. So when he forced the capitulation of Jerusalem, his cause and his gods seemed vindicated. It was in demonstration of that conviction that he brought the gold and silver articles that had been dedicated to the service of Jehovah in Jerusalem to Babylon to be placed in the treasure house of his gods. The heathen gods had triumphed! Nebuchadnezzar was sovereign!

In this case, as in so many other historical situations, appearances were deceiving. Actually, Jehovah was as much in charge of the overthrow of Jerusalem as he had been many times earlier in its defense. In fact, it was Jehovah who had brought on the destruction, sending it as a punishment for the people's sins. Now, in spite of the fact that he had "delivered Jehoiakim into [Nebuchadnezzar's] hand," God was going to show that he was sovereign.

Gleason L. Archer, whose commentary in the *Expositor's Bible Commentary* is one of the best works on Daniel available today, puts it like this:

> The principal theological emphasis in Daniel is the absolute sovereignty of Yahweh, the God of Israel. At a time when it seemed to all the world that his cause was lost and that the gods of the heathen had triumphed, causing his temple to be burned to the ground, it pleased the Lord strikingly and unmistakably to display his omnipotence. The theme running through the whole book is that the fortunes of kings and the affairs of men are subject to God's decrees, and that he is able to accomplish his will despite the most determined opposition of the mightiest potentates on earth.
>
> The miracles recorded in chapters 1–6 demonstrate God's sovereignty on behalf of his saints. The surpassing health of Daniel and his three companions after ten days of a simple vegetable diet (ch. 1); the miraculous disclosure to Daniel of the contents of Nebuchadnezzar's dream (ch. 2); the amazing deliverance of Daniel's three friends from the fiery furnace (ch. 3); the previous warning to Nebuchadnezzar of seven years of dehumanizing insanity because of his overweening pride (ch. 4); the terrifying prediction inscribed on the banquet wall of Belshazzar, followed by a speedy fulfillment of the same (ch. 5); and Daniel's deliverance from the lions' den all clearly show that the Lord God of Israel was in charge of the tide of human affairs and was perfectly able to deliver his people from pagan oppression during their captivity.[4]

The great and most important theme of Daniel is that there is but one God, who is Jehovah, and that he is sovereign over the events of history.

A Tale of Two Cities

Yet this needs to be placed in an even larger context. One of the most influential books on theology ever written is *The City of God* by Saint Augustine of Hippo (written between A.D. 412 and 426). Its theme concerns the existence of two societies, which Augustine calls "cities." One is God's society. The other is the society of this world. Augustine described them, saying, "Two cities have been formed by two loves: the earthly by the love of self, even to the contempt of God; the heavenly by the love of God, even to the contempt of self."[5]

The reason I mention Augustine's theology of history at this point is that much of his discussion concerns the contrast between Babylon, which he sees as a spectacular embodiment of the earthly city, and earthly Jerusalem, which he sees as a symbol of the city of God. This is a proper emphasis, and it is important here because it reminds us that the struggle between Nebuchadnezzar and God, recorded in Daniel, is actually only one example of that greater struggle between the world's way of doing things and God's way of doing things, which has prevailed at all times and prevails today. It is this that makes Daniel a contemporary book.

The chief characteristic of Babylon in Nebuchadnezzar's time was what we would call its radical secular humanism. I say this because of a statement Nebuchadnezzar makes later on in Daniel, in the fourth chapter: "Is not this the great Babylon I have built as the royal residence, by my mighty power and for the glory of my majesty?" (Dan. 4:30). This is a true statement in one sense. Nebuchadnezzar had built Babylon, and he had undoubtedly done it for his own glory. But in forgetting God, who had given him the opportunity to create such magnificence, Nebuchadnezzar was actually taking God's glory to himself. Like all secular humanists, he was saying that all that exists is *of* man, *by* man, and *for* man's glory. That is a true expression of the earthly city.

In twentieth-century America secularism is noticeable in many ways, as people increasingly view reality as emerging from man and as existing for man and his glory. Let me give two examples.

First, there is the philosophy of evolution, which is the dominant reference for most persons' thinking and which extends to almost everything. Why is evolution so popular, and why are our educators so insistent that it and only it must be taught in our schools? There are different reasons for evolution's popularity, of course. For one thing, according to evolutionary theory, everything is knowable since everything stands in a direct causal relationship to everything else and may be traced backward or forward through those relationships. This has obvious appeal. Second, reality has only one explanation: The fittest survive, whether a biological mutation, a government, or an ideal. Third—and I think this is the chief reason—evolution eliminates God, precisely what Nebuchadnezzar was trying to do in his own way. If all things can be explained as the natural outworking or development of previous causes, then God may be safely banished to an otherworldly kingdom or even be eliminated altogether, as many, even so-called theologians, have done. Evolution allows man to be the center of the universe.

The second example of today's secularism is our current doctrine of the separation of church and state, which comes into a study of Daniel if for no other reason than that the struggle of Nebuchadnezzar, who represents the state, against God is so prominent. The doctrine of the separation of church and state used to mean that each functioned separately, kings or presidents not being allowed to appoint clerical authorities or run the church, and clerical authorities not being allowed to appoint kings or presidents. Nevertheless, it was always understood that both church and state were responsible to God, in whose wisdom each had been established. They were two independent servants of one master. Although neither was permitted to rule the other, each was to remind the other of its God-appointed duties and recall it to upright, godly conduct if it should stray.

Today, however, the doctrine of the separation of church and state is taken, often by church people, to mean that the church is irrelevant to the state—though the state increasingly brings its secular philosophy to bear on the church. Thus Christians withdraw from politics and neglect even to inform themselves of national or international issues. As a result, the articulation of spiritual and moral principles is eliminated from debates. The state becomes its own god with its chief operating principle being paganism. For its part, the state deliberately tries to keep religious values out of politics, promising to protect the right to worship so long as those wanting to worship do so *on the reservation*. The one thing Christians and other religious people must not do is attempt to bring their convictions out of this isolation ward into the real world.

I have always felt that modern secularism is expressed well in Algernon Charles Swinburne's "Hymn of Man."

> But God, if a God there be, is the
>   Substance of men which is Man.
> Thou art smitten, thou God, thou art smitten;
>   Thy death is upon thee, O Lord.
> And the love-song of earth as thou diest
>   Resounds through the wind of her wings—
> Glory to Man in the highest!
> For man is the master of things.[6]

This is the way the world's city always thinks. Nebuchadnezzar considered himself master because he was able to take gold and silver out of the Jerusalem treasury and carry them to Babylon. Cain, which is where the secular city began, considered himself master because he had the strength and cunning to kill Abel. Rome considered itself master because its legions were able to march unhindered across the ancient world.

But the world is not master. God is master. God is sovereign, and he is able to bring the secular city down. He did it in the case of Nebuchadnezzar, as the story of Daniel shows. Nebuchadnezzar judged himself superior to all around him because of his military triumphs and achievements. He thought he had no need for God. But God declared, "This is what is decreed for you, King Nebuchadnezzar: Your royal authority has been taken from you. You will be driven away from people and will live with the wild animals; you will eat grass like cattle. Seven times will pass by for you until you acknowledge that the Most High is sovereign over the kingdoms of men and gives them to anyone he wishes" (Dan. 4:31–32).

That is what happened. Nebuchadnezzar became insane and was driven from the city. The text says, "Immediately what had been said about Nebuchadnezzar was fulfilled. He was driven away from people and ate grass like cattle. His body was drenched with the dew of heaven until his hair grew like the feathers of an eagle and his nails like the claws of a bird" (v. 33).

This is what happens when people take the glory of God to themselves. They lose the proper glory they should have, that of having been made in God's image, and they become like beasts. Indeed, they become worse than beasts—because beasts, when they are beastlike, are at least behaving the way beasts should behave, while we, by contrast, commit crimes of which they cannot even conceive.

The People of God

At the same time, while the world is living by its own standards and for its own glory in opposition to God, there is another people who know God and honestly try to please him. In this story they are Daniel and his friends. They are not the most visible people, just as the city they represent is not nearly so visible as the city of this world. But they are substantial people. And in the final analysis they are the only ones who make any real difference for good.

Are you with Daniel? Are you a member of his special band? No one is by nature in the company of these servants of the true God. All are born into the secular city. But the city of God can be entered by new birth through faith in the Lord Jesus Christ as Savior. Jesus said, "No one can see the kingdom of God unless he is born again" (John 3:3). The doors of that city stand open for any who will enter it. The New Testament says of Abraham, another citizen of the heavenly city who lived for God in the secular city, "By faith he made his home in the promised land like a stranger in a foreign country; he lived in tents, as did Isaac and Jacob, who were heirs with him of the same promise. For he was looking forward to the city with foundations, whose architect and builder is God" (Heb. 11:9–10).

If you are not a member of the city of God, I invite you to become one now through faith in Jesus Christ, and then begin to live here in a way that makes the invisible kingdom visible to many.[7]

2

A Young Man Decides

Daniel 1:3–21

Then the king ordered Ashpenaz, chief of his court officials, to bring in some of the Israelites from the royal family and the nobility—young men without any physical defect, handsome, showing aptitude for every kind of learning, well informed, quick to understand, and qualified to serve in the king's palace. He was to teach them the language and literature of the Babylonians. The king assigned them a daily amount of food and wine from the king's table. They were to be trained for three years, and after that they were to enter the king's service.

Among these were some from Judah: Daniel, Hananiah, Mishael and Azariah. The chief official gave them new names: to Daniel, the name Belteshazzar; to Hananiah, Shadrach; to Mishael, Meshach; and to Azariah, Abednego.

But Daniel resolved not to defile himself with the royal food and wine.

At the time of the Protestant Reformation, the two greatest reformers, Martin Luther and John Calvin, each issued commentaries on Daniel. Luther produced two studies, published in 1524 and 1544. Calvin produced one, published in 1561. It is a striking fact that in spite of Luther's great popularity, which continues to this day, Luther's books on Daniel have never been translated into English, while Calvin's massive work, running to a thousand pages in the original Latin, was available in English within ten years.

Why has the text of Calvin's commentary proved so popular? There may be many reasons, but most people feel that it is because of the passionate

19

and moving way in which the great expositor linked the times of the exiled Daniel to his own.

Calvin lived in an age of ecclesiastical and political warfare in which many thousands suffered greatly for their faith. In Germany in 1546, Charles V began a war to stamp out Lutheranism. In France, between 1540 and 1544, Francis I attempted the same thing, massacring the Waldensians as part of his misconceived program. In 1545 he burned twenty-two villages and killed three thousand men and women. Others were sent to the galleys. In 1562, the year after Calvin's commentary appeared, the eight Wars of Religion began, the destruction of which was so great that Europe did not recover for two centuries. Thousands became exiles during this period. Many fled to Switzerland where Calvin, who was himself an exile, lived.

Calvin's commentary breathes with compassion for these people, and as a result it has always appealed to those who consider themselves exiles in a strange land. Indeed, it appears even more broadly than this. For Daniel was a man of God in worldly Babylon, and Christians are always God's people in the midst of those who do not honor and in fact oppose their divine King.

Calvin dedicated his book to the "pious Protestants of France" and urged Daniel upon them as a great encouragement.

> I have the very best occasion of showing you, beloved brethren, in this mirror, how God proves the faith of his people in these days by various trials; and how with wonderful wisdom he has taken care to strengthen their minds by ancient examples, that they should never be weakened by the concussion of the severest storms and tempests; or at least, if they should totter at all, that they should never finally fall away. For although the servants of God are required to run in a course impeded by many obstacles, yet whoever diligently reads this book will find in it whatever is needed by a voluntary and active runner to guide him from the starting point to the goal; while good and strenuous wrestlers will experimentally acknowledge that they have been sufficiently prepared for the contest. . . . Here then, we observe, as in a living picture, that when God spares and even indulges the wicked for a time, he proves his servants like gold and silver; so that we ought not to consider it a grievance to be thrown into the furnace of trial, while profane men enjoy the calmness of repose.[1]

A Secular Environment

In order to understand Daniel we must realize that the Babylon to which Daniel and his three friends were taken was a secular, worldly place, as I attempted to show in the last study, and that their initial experiences there were intended to blot out of their minds the remembrance of the true God and their homeland. We see this in several ways. For one thing, Nebuchadnezzar ordered Ashpenaz, chief of his court officials, to choose young men who would be easily molded by their new environment. Again, he attempted to lure them with the delicacies of food the great city of Babylon could provide.

Chiefly we notice Nebuchadnezzar's intentions in the altering of the young men's names. The Hebrew names of these young men were Daniel, Hananiah, Mishael, and Azariah. They were changed to Belteshazzar, Shadrach, Meshach, and Abednego. It should be immediately evident to anyone with even a limited knowledge of Hebrew that the Jewish names of these men each contains a name of God and has a spiritual meaning. Daniel and Mishael both contain the syllable *el,* which means "God" and is the basis of the frequently appearing (plural) name *Elohim.* Daniel means "God is my Judge." Mishael means "Who is like God?" The other two names, Hananiah and Azariah, both contain a shortened form of the name Jehovah. Hananiah means "Jehovah is gracious." Azariah means "Jehovah is my helper." The very names of these men were reminders of their heritage and a challenge to them to remain faithful to the Lord. But now, deported into a strange, pagan land, their names are changed. And the names they are given all contain a reference to one of the false gods of the ancient Babylonians, Aku and Nego. It was a way of saying that these who had been servants of the Jewish God were now servants and worshipers of the gods of the pagan pantheon.

Yet the change accomplished nothing. Nebuchadnezzar changed the men's names, but he could not change their hearts. They remained faithful to the true God of Israel, as the story shows.

I apply that to our own age. One thing the world seems always to try to do—it has happened in the past, and it is happening in our own time—is to take Christian words and rework them to convey the world's ideas. I suppose it is one of the devil's subtlest tricks. It happens in liberal theology. "Sin" used to mean rebellion against God and his righteous law or, as the Westminster Shorter Catechism puts it, "any want of conformity unto, or transgression of, the law of God" (A. 14). But today it means ignorance or merely the kind of oppression that is supposed to reside in social structures. "Jesus" is no longer the incarnate God who died for our salvation, but rather our example or what might even be termed an evolutionary peak of the human race. "Faith" is awareness of oppression and beginning to do something about it, and so on. Of course, in the secular world the readjustment of words is even more ridiculous and extreme, as the recent use of the term "born again" in advertising slogans shows.

This is a great danger, I admit. But although it is a danger, if the truth of what is behind these words remains strong in the minds and hearts of those who really know the truth, then the vitality of the faith will remain regardless of the world's corruptions. Christians will persevere because God will strengthen them to stand against the culture.

Daniel's Decision

The most important verse in the first chapter of Daniel is verse 8, which says, "But Daniel resolved not to defile himself with the royal food and wine."

What is your reaction to that? Remember that Daniel was a young man at this time. We know from the later development of the story that he lived for a very long time beyond this—through the rule of four emperors. He was probably in his nineties when he died. So at this point he was probably between fifteen and seventeen. It was at this young age that he was taken away from his own country and culture, plunged into the strange but exciting life of the great world capital, and lured to loyalty by the best of all possible educations and by provision of the very food served to Nebuchadnezzar. Yet Daniel refused to partake of this food. As I say, what is your reaction to that? Do you find it a very little thing? Do you see Daniel's decision as the immaturity and foolishness of youth? Would you have acted as Daniel and his friends did in these circumstances, or would you have gone along with your great benefactor's desires? Would you have said, "After all, why should we live by Jewish dietary laws while in Babylon? Let's eat and drink. It's just a small thing"?

Well, it was a small thing. Yet that is just the point. For it is in the small matters that great victories are won. This is where decisions to live a holy life are made—not in the big things (though they come if the little things are neglected), but in the details of life. If Daniel had said, "I want to live for God in big ways, but I am not going to make a fool of myself in this trivial matter of eating and drinking the king's food," he never would have amounted to anything. But because he started out for God in small things, God used him greatly.

I have titled this chapter "A Young Man Decides" because it is particularly in youth that the most significant and life-forming decisions are made. Are you a young person? Then you should pay particularly close attention to this point. Most young people want their lives to count, and most Christian young people want their lives to count for God. Youth dreams big. That is right. You should dream big. But youth is also often impatient and undisciplined, and young people are tempted to let the little things slide. You must not do that if you are God's young man or God's young woman. God will make your life count, but this will not happen unless you determine to live for him in the little things now. You know what Jesus said: "Whoever can be trusted with very little can also be trusted with much, and whoever is dishonest with very little will also be dishonest with much" (Luke 16:10). Being wholly given over to God now is the essential and best possible preparation for future service.

Why We Must Be Holy

In the last chapter I pointed out that Daniel is a story of the struggle of the world's people and culture against God's people and God's culture, and it is. But it is also a story of men who lived for God by choosing the path of personal discipleship and holiness. This is no contradiction, because it is only such persons who actually embody the spiritual standards of "the city of God." It is only these who make any lasting difference in the world.

A great evangelical bishop of England, John Charles Ryle, wrote a classic study of holiness in which he urged holiness upon all who call themselves Christians. After some opening passages in which he describes holiness as separation to God, devotion to God, service to God, being of one mind with God and wanting God's will—Ryle went on to show why holiness, the kind of holiness exercised by Daniel, is so necessary. He listed eight reasons.

1. "We must be holy, because *the voice of God in Scripture plainly commands it.*" Peter wrote, "As obedient children, do not conform to the evil desires you had when you lived in ignorance. But just as he who called you is holy, so be holy in all you do; for it is written: 'Be holy, because I am holy'" (1 Peter 1:14–16). This is not optional. God did not say, "I would like you to live a holy life; but if you are not too excited about that particular lifestyle, don't worry about it. We'll work on something else." God said, "Be holy, because I am holy." We must be holy because the holy God commands it.

2. "We must be holy, because *this is the one grand end and purpose for which Christ came into the world.*" You say, "But I thought Jesus came to save us from our sins." Yes, he did come for that. But the Bible also says, "Christ loved the church and gave himself up for her to make her holy, cleansing her by the washing with water through the word, and to present her to himself as a radiant church, without stain or wrinkle or any other blemish, but holy and blameless" (Eph. 5:25–27). Many Christians think they would like the benefits of salvation without the obligation to live for Christ, but they cannot have them because Christ came to make them holy just as much as he came to save them from the penalty of their sins. If you are fighting against holiness, you are fighting against nothing less than the purpose of God in the Atonement.

3. "We must be holy, because *this is the only sound evidence that we have a saving faith in our Lord Jesus Christ.*" How is that so? Well, James in his letter speaks of two kinds of faith: a living, saving faith and a dead faith that saves no one. The devils have a dead faith; that is, they believe there is a God and that Jesus is his Son, sent to save his people. But they do not trust him personally. They do not live for him. A living faith does live for him and therefore shows itself in good works. That is why James says, "As the body without the spirit is dead, so faith without deeds is dead" (James 2:26).

Ryle used this point to comment on so-called "death-bed" conversions, judging that in ninety-nine cases out of a hundred these "conversions" are illusory. He said, "With rare exceptions, men die just as they have lived. The only safe evidence that we are one with Christ, and Christ is in us, is a holy life."[2]

4. "We must be holy, because *this is the only proof that we love the Lord Jesus Christ in sincerity.*" Jesus was quite plain on this point. He said, "If you love me, you will obey what I command" (John 14:15); "Whoever has my commands and obeys them, he is the one who loves me" (v. 21); "If anyone loves me, he will obey my teaching" (v. 23); "You are my friends if you do what I

command" (John 15:14). How could the point be more clearly spoken? If you love Jesus, you will obey him; you will be holy. If you do not obey him, you do not love him—whatever your profession. Do you love Jesus? We have a chorus in which we sing, "Oh, how I love Jesus," but you do not love him if you do not do what he says.

5. "We must be holy, because *this is the only sound evidence that we are true children of God.*" Do you remember how Jesus made this point when he was talking with the Pharisees? They claimed to be children of Abraham and therefore in right standing before God. But Jesus said, "If you were Abraham's children, then you would do the things Abraham did" (John 8:39–40). Paul said the same thing in Romans, noting that "those who are led by the Spirit of God are sons of God" (Rom. 8:14). The Spirit of God does not lead you to sin. The Spirit of God does not lead to disobedience. If you are led by God's Spirit, you will lead a holy life, and the evidence of that holy life will be sound evidence that you are God's son or daughter.

6. "We must be holy, because *this is the most likely way to do good to others.*" Many people today have some desire to do good to others, and many of our social and benevolence programs are an expression of that praiseworthy desire. But I ask, "Do you help others by advancing a low moral standard— one that is easy for them to live up to? Do you help others by whittling down the righteous standards of the Old Testament law or the New Testament precepts? Not at all! You help others by upholding the highest possible standards and above all by living according to those standards yourself. There are several places in the New Testament in which the godly conduct of a believer is said to be the best hope of doing good to someone else. For instance, Peter writes, "Wives, . . . be submissive to your husbands so that, if any of them do not believe the word, they may be won over without words by the behavior of their wives, when they see the purity and reverence of your lives" (1 Peter 3:1–2). No doubt many besides husbands have been won to Christ by the consistent, holy behavior of some Christian.

7. "We must be holy, because *our present comfort depends much upon it.*" Not all suffering is directly related to a suffering person's sin. Christ's words about the man born blind (John 9:3) should disabuse us of attempts to make that an easy, one-to-one relationship. But although all suffering does not come directly from one's sin, the reverse is true: All sin produces suffering.

We do not think this way naturally. In fact, we think just the opposite. We come up against one of God's commandments, think that we would like to do something else, and immediately reason that if only we could do what we really want to do we would be happy. We think that we would be absolutely miserable obeying God. That was the devil's argument in his temptation of Eve, but it is as diabolical now as it was then. To heed it is to forget whence our good comes. "Every good and perfect gift is from above, coming down from the Father of the heavenly lights, who does not change like shifting shadows" (James 1:17). If we turn from this good, we do not turn to happiness but away from it.

8. "Lastly, we must be holy, because *without holiness on earth we shall never be prepared to enjoy heaven.*" The author of Hebrews wrote, "Without holiness no one will see the Lord" (Heb. 12:14). Revelation speaks of heaven, saying, "Nothing impure will ever enter it, nor will anyone who does what is shameful or deceitful, but only those whose names are written in the Lamb's book of life" (Rev. 21:27).[3]

Can I Be Holy?

The objection I am likely to get is that these points are all very well and good but that it is just not possible for you to live a holy life in your circumstances. "If I did the right thing in my job, I'd lose it," you say. Or, "None of my friends would speak to me." Or, "I'd never get ahead." Or, "I just can't be holy; I've tried it and I fail."

If you are thinking this way, let me turn back to Daniel, who was not only resolved not to defile himself with the king's food and wine but was also willing to put the matter to the test and prove God able in his circumstances. Daniel said to the guard who had been appointed over him, "Please test your servants for ten days: Give us nothing but vegetables to eat and water to drink. Then compare our appearance with that of the young men who eat the royal food, and treat your servants in accordance with what you see" (Dan. 1:12–13).

The guard agreed to this test, and at the end of the ten days the young men looked healthier and better nourished than any of the young men who ate the royal food. Moreover, it was not only in their appearance that Daniel, Hananiah, Mishael, and Azariah excelled. They also excelled in knowledge and understanding of all kinds of literature and learning. The text concludes by noting that at the end of the three years of training, when the king brought his young protégés in for testing, Nebuchadnezzar "found them ten times better than all the magicians and enchanters in his whole kingdom" (v. 20).

Do not say, "If I live for God, I'll lose out." You may lose out on some of the things the world offers, which are not good for you anyway, but you will experience a richness of God's bounty. The Bible says, "Seek first [God's] kingdom and [God's] righteousness, and all these things will be given to you as well" (Matt. 6:33).

3

God of the Nations

Daniel 2:1-23

Then Daniel praised the God of heaven and said:

> *"Praise be to the name of God for ever and ever;*
> *wisdom and power are his.*
> *He changes times and seasons;*
> *he sets up kings and deposes them.*
> *He gives wisdom to the wise*
> *and knowledge to the discerning.*
> *He reveals deep and hidden things;*
> *he knows what lies in darkness,*
> *and light dwells with him.*
> *I thank and praise you, O God of my fathers:*
> *You have given me wisdom and power,*
> *you have made known to me what we asked of you,*
> *you have made known to us the dream of the king."*

At the end of Daniel 1 we are told that God gave Daniel three things. Because of his decision not to defile himself with the food and culture of the Babylonians, God granted Daniel *wisdom* beyond the wisdom of the Babylonians, *influence* beyond that of any in the kingdom, and *health* that resulted in long life. However, when we move from the end of the first to

26

the beginning of the second chapter, we find that each of these is at once either disregarded or threatened.

At the end of his period of training, Daniel was presumably graduated into the company of wise men and statesmen referred to by Nebuchadnezzar as "the magicians, enchanters, sorcerers and astrologers" (Dan. 2:2). But we need to remember that he was still only about eighteen or nineteen years of age and that there were undoubtedly many among those men who were far greater and far more influential than he was. They had been advisers to the emperors of Babylon for many years. In that company Daniel would have been "low man on the pole." Indeed, when Nebuchadnezzar had his dream, which is the central episode of this chapter, an inquiry about it was made to these men. But Daniel did not seem to have been consulted and, in fact, did not even know what was happening until the order was given to execute the wise men. So Daniel had no power and negligible influence. And so far as health and long life are concerned, we find that when the wise men were unable to tell the king what his dream was and the king threatened to kill them all, Daniel, who was not even consulted and whose influence in ancient Babylon did not amount to a hill of beans at this time, was nevertheless also on the verge of extermination.

However, although his gifts were disregarded and although he was now under sentence of death by Nebuchadnezzar, Daniel *was* wise and the crisis became the occasion through which God brought him to the forefront of leadership.

God brought Daniel to the fore! That is worth repeating, because here as elsewhere in the story we see the overriding sovereignty of God in this young man's affairs. In fact, the sovereignty of God is the connection between these chapters. In chapter 1 God gave Daniel wisdom, influence, and health or long life. Now, in spite of the threat to kill Daniel, God fulfills what he has promised. How? By being sovereign over the details of history, which is the book's theme. If God does not control our lives—from the actions of kings and others in positions of power to the most minute circumstances—then everything in life is uncertain. We are victims of circumstances, and whatever happens will happen. *Que sera, sera!* But if God is sovereign, as the Bible declares him to be, and if he is our God—if the promises he makes and the actions he takes are certain of fulfillment—then we can be confident of the future and know that we will be able to live our lives in a way that will please God.

The King Dreamed a Dream

"In the second year of his reign, Nebuchadnezzar had dreams; his mind was troubled and he could not sleep" (Dan. 2:1). Nebuchadnezzar was not the first monarch in history to dream troublesome dreams. Nor was he the last. Statesmen are often troubled by the past and have forebodings about the future. But Nebuchadnezzar's dream was not like the dreams that normal statesmen have. Nebuchadnezzar's dream had been given to him by God, even though he did not know who this God was; and because it had been given to him by God, it was an accurate revelation. It was prophecy of important events to come.

Unfortunately, Nebuchadnezzar could not remember his dream.

But he had people around him who were supposed to be able to deal with such things. So he called the magicians, enchanters, sorcerers, and astrologers together and announced, "I have had a dream that troubles me and I want to know what it means" (v. 3).

The astrologers said, "O king, live forever! Tell your servants the dream, and we will interpret it" (v. 4).

It is worth a digression here to observe that beginning with this verse (2:4) the Book of Daniel changes from being written in Hebrew, which has been the case up to this point, to Aramaic, which continues to the end of chapter 7. For the most part the Old Testament was written in Hebrew and the New Testament in Greek. But there are a few exceptions, and this is one of them. Why is this important? For one thing, it suggests that the earlier portion of the book (chapters 2–7), which deals with things that happened to Daniel and his friends in Babylon, concerns Babylon and was therefore recorded in a language that would make it available to the people of that land, while the latter portion of the book (chapters 8–12), which concerns the future of the Jewish people, was written in their official language. In other words, Daniel expresses God's concern for both peoples.

But there is more to it than that. After the Jews returned from Babylon, the common language of the people was Aramaic, which they learned during the seventy years of exile, and the use of two languages by Daniel is therefore a strong argument for the genuineness of the book. No one writing at a later date would have written part of the book in one language and part in another. A late imposter would have written it exclusively in Aramaic. An earlier imposter would have written it in Hebrew. But only a man who spoke Hebrew but who had learned Aramaic in the Babylonian court would have written the part of the book that dealt with Babylon in Aramaic so that it could be understood by Babylonians, and part in Hebrew so that it would fit in with the rest of the Jewish Scriptures.

At any rate, the astrologers answered the king *in Aramaic*, saying, "Tell us the dream, and we will interpret it."

Nebuchadnezzar ignored their request and repeated what he had said originally, but with the addition of a threat if they did not tell him the dream and its interpretation. "This is what I have firmly decided: If you do not tell me what my dream was and interpret it, I will have you cut into pieces and your houses turned into piles of rubble. But if you tell me the dream and explain it, you will receive from me gifts and rewards and great honor. So tell me the dream and interpret it for me" (Dan. 2:5–6).

At this point we are probably to detect a rising note of dismay in the wise men's voices. "Let the king tell his servants the dream, and we will interpret it" (v. 7).

Have you ever been in an interview when the conversation went from bad to worse? That is what seems to have happened here. Each side had a reasonable position. The astrologers argued that they could not tell what the dream meant unless the king told them what the dream was, and the king replied that if they were true astrologers and not fakes, they should be able to divine what he had dreamed. This was going nowhere quickly. Nebuchadnezzar said, "I am certain that you are trying to gain time, because you realize that this is what I have firmly decided: If you do not tell me the dream, there is just one penalty for you. You have conspired to tell me misleading and wicked things, hoping the situation will change. So then, tell me the dream, and I will know that you can interpret it for me" (vv. 8–9).

The astrologers replied, "There is not a man on earth who can do what the king asks! No king, however great and mighty, has ever asked such a thing of any magician or enchanter or astrologer. What the king asks is too difficult. No one can reveal it to the king except the gods, and they do not live among men" (vv. 10–11).

Is that not interesting? "No one can reveal it to the king except the gods," said these astrologers. No, but there was one true God who does reveal himself to men, who would later say through Amos, "Surely the Sovereign LORD does nothing without revealing his plan to his servants the prophets" (Amos 3:7). In this case, God would reveal what he was about to do through Daniel. The stage was set for the first great revelation to Nebuchadnezzar of the reality, wisdom, and power of the one true God.

Effectual, Fervent Prayer

Daniel had not been party to this first confrontation, as I said. He was too much of a junior wise man to be invited. But when the command went out to execute the astrologers, Daniel was nevertheless included. And it was not long before Arioch, the commander of the king's guard, came to escort Daniel and his friends to death row.

At this point Daniel reveals an astonishing measure of faith—particularly for a young man. He went to the king and asked for time, so that he might interpret the dream for him. Where did Daniel get faith in God strong enough to make such an offer? No doubt Daniel and his friends were well-versed in the Old Testament Scriptures, and they undoubtedly knew the story of Joseph and his interpretation of the dreams of the chief butler and chief cupbearer of Pharaoh and the important dream of Pharaoh. Their situation in Babylon was comparable to Joseph's. Moreover, when Daniel appeared before Nebuchadnezzar to explain the dream, he answered as Joseph had answered Pharaoh, giving full glory to God: "No wise man, enchanter, magician or diviner can explain to the king the mystery he has

asked about, but there is a God in heaven who reveals mysteries" (Dan.
2:27–28; cf. Gen. 41:16, 25). Still, the circumstances were not entirely the
same, because Pharaoh had remembered his dream and could tell it to Joseph
while Nebuchadnezzar had forgotten his dream and could not tell it to Daniel.
Humanly speaking, the situation for Daniel was more difficult.

But only humanly speaking! For man it was an impossible situation. But
for God it was no more difficult to disclose and interpret this dream than
it was merely to interpret the first. The secret of Daniel's great faith and
power is that he had his eyes on God. Like Peter, who walked toward Jesus
over the churning water of the Sea of Galilee, Daniel had fixed his eyes on
God, and he did not doubt that God could both disclose the dream and
give its meaning.

That night Daniel called a prayer meeting, and the "effectual, fervent
prayer" of these four righteous men availed much. God revealed the dream
to Daniel, and the next day Daniel revealed and interpreted the dream to
King Nebuchadnezzar.

To God Be the Glory

If we were telling the story, we might rush directly to the interpretation
of Nebuchadnezzar's dream at this point. But instead Daniel gives us the
prayer he made upon waking. Why is this inserted? One answer is that it is
undoubtedly a true record of what happened. Daniel was so struck by God's
goodness in answering his prayer and that of his friends that he could not
escape praising God for it. Calvin wrote, "Whenever God confers any remarkable blessing on his servants, they are the more stirred up to praise him."[1]
That is one reason.

But the theme of the prayer is also the theme of these opening chapters:
the sovereignty of God, as I said. Therefore, it is a commentary on why Daniel
had been able to act as he had acted and what the dream, which is yet to be
interpreted, will be about.

The prayer has three parts.

First, there is praise to God for two of his most important attributes: wisdom and power. This means that the prayer begins with adoration, as all
good prayers do. How appropriate is the ascription of wisdom to God in
these circumstances! The Babylon of this day was the seat of earthly wisdom,
and Daniel and his friends had been brought to Babylon to be trained in
that wisdom. However, in the story that leads up to this, the wisdom of the
wisest of the Babylonians, the magicians, enchanters, sorcerers, and
astrologers, had shown to be inadequate. They had confessed, "There
is not a man on earth who can do what the king asks. . . . What the king asks
is too difficult. No one can reveal it to the king except the gods" (vv. 10–11).
That was true. But there is a God in whom is hidden all wisdom, and this is
disclosed in the story.

In his classic book *The Knowledge of the Holy*, A. W. Tozer has a chapter called "The Wisdom of God," in which he says,

> The idea of God as infinitely wise is at the root of all truth. It is a datum of belief necessary to the soundness of all other beliefs about God. . . . Wisdom, among other things, is the ability to devise perfect ends and to achieve those ends by the most perfect means. It sees the end from the beginning, so there can be no need to guess or conjecture. Wisdom sees everything in focus, each in proper relation to all, and is thus able to work toward predestined goals with flawless precision. All God's acts are done in perfect wisdom, first for his own glory, and then for the highest good of the greatest number for the longest time. And all his acts are as pure as they are wise, and as good as they are wise and pure. Not only could his acts not be better done: a better way to do them could not be imagined. An infinitely wise God must work in a manner not to be improved upon by finite creatures. O Lord, how manifold are thy works! In wisdom hast thou made them all. The earth is full of thy riches.[2]

The second attribute for which Daniel praised God is power, that is, his sovereignty, the theme of the book. I often point out when teaching about sovereignty that in our natural state none of us likes this attribute of God. This is because we want to be sovereign ourselves. We want to be powerful, to control our lives. This was true of Nebuchadnezzar. As the story develops, we are going to see that the battle between Nebuchadnezzar and God was over this issue precisely. Who was in control? Was it Nebuchadnezzar, the greatest ruler of the time? Nebuchadnezzar, who held the very lives of his subjects in his hands? Or was it God, whom Nebuchadnezzar would not even acknowledge? As the story unfolds, Nebuchadnezzar at length subjects himself to this God and confesses openly,

> His dominion is an eternal dominion;
>   his kingdom endures from generation to generation.
> All the peoples of the earth
>   are regarded as nothing.
> He does as he pleases
>   with the power of heaven
>   and the peoples of the earth.
> No one can hold back his hand
>   or say to him: "What have you done?"
>
> Daniel 4:34–35

The second part of Daniel's prayer is the acknowledgment that, although all wisdom and power are God's, God nevertheless imparts both wisdom and power to mankind. He imparts power, for "he changes times and seasons; he sets up kings and deposes them" (Dan. 2:21). He imparts wisdom, for "he gives wisdom to the wise and knowledge to the discerning. He reveals deep and hidden things; he knows what lies in darkness, and light dwells with him"

(vv. 21–22). No doubt the greatest portion of this wisdom, wisdom of spiritual things, is reserved for God's people alone. The Bible declares, "The man without the Spirit does not accept the things that come from the Spirit of God, for they are foolishness to him, and he cannot understand them, because they are spiritually discerned" (1 Cor. 2:14). But there is a general wisdom given to nonbelievers too, just as political power is given to nonbelieving as well as believing rulers. The important thing is the recognition that this comes from God, which Daniel did recognize but which Nebuchadnezzar, at least at this stage in his life, did not. It makes all the difference in the way we live our lives when we know that God and not man is ultimately in charge of these circumstances.

Finally, in the third part of his prayer Daniel praises God for the wisdom and power he had imparted to him personally:

> I thank and praise you, O God of my fathers:
>   You have given me wisdom and power,
> you have made known to me what we asked of you,
>   you have made known to us the dream of the king.
>
> Daniel 2:23

You and I have not been given Daniel's special ability to know and understand dreams because God does not speak this way today. But wise as Daniel was, we have a wisdom greater even than his since it has been given to us to know and believe on Jesus Christ personally. The Bible says that in Christ "are hidden all the treasures of wisdom and knowledge" (Col. 2:3). So to know Jesus as Savior and Lord is to be wise. If you have that knowledge, do you thank God for it, as Daniel did? Do you praise him for the wisdom that has made you wise unto salvation?

4

Rock of Ages

Daniel 2:24–49

You, O king, are the king of kings. The God of heaven has given you dominion and power and might and glory; in your hands he has placed mankind and the beasts of the field and the birds of the air. Wherever they live, he has made you ruler over them all. You are that head of gold.

After you, another kingdom will rise, inferior to yours. Next, a third kingdom, one of bronze, will rule over the whole earth. Finally, there will be a fourth kingdom, strong as iron—for iron breaks and smashes everything—and as iron breaks things to pieces, so it will crush and break all the others. Just as you saw that the feet and toes were partly of baked clay and partly of iron, so this will be a divided kingdom; yet it will have some of the strength of iron in it, even as you saw iron mixed with clay. As the toes were partly iron and partly clay, so this kingdom will be partly strong and partly brittle. And just as you saw the iron mixed with baked clay, so the people will be a mixture and will not remain united, any more than iron mixes with clay.

In the time of those kings, the God of heaven will set up a kingdom that will never be destroyed, nor will it be left to another people. It will crush all those kingdoms and bring them to an end, but it will itself endure forever. This is the meaning of the vision of the rock cut out of a mountain, but not by human hands—a rock that broke the iron, the bronze, the clay, the silver and the gold to pieces.

The great God has shown the king what will take place in the future. The dream is true and the interpretation is trustworthy.

The Book of Daniel is a magnificent story of the triumph of Daniel and three other godly men in the midst of the moral and spiritual miasma of ancient Babylon. But it is also a record of important visions that prophesy both immediate and distant historical events. The fact that the visions of Daniel prophesy these events so clearly is one reason critical scholars of the Old Testament have been hard on Daniel. They cannot believe that God could have given his servant revelations of actual historical events to come. Nevertheless, this is what God did, and it is to the first of these prophetic visions that we come now.

Nebuchadnezzar had dreamed an important dream. But he had forgotten it, and the dream was disclosed only after Daniel and his friends had prayed for God to reveal it to them.

As Daniel explained it, Nebuchadnezzar had dreamed about "a large statue—an enormous, dazzling statue, awesome in appearance" (Dan. 2:31). It was made of different kinds of metal. The head of the statue was of gold. The chest and arms were of silver. The middle portions of the statue were of bronze. The legs were of iron, and the feet were of iron mixed with baked clay. While the king was watching, a rock that was not "cut out . . . by human hands" struck the statue on its feet, and the whole thing toppled over and broke in pieces, the pieces then being swept away by the wind like chaff at threshing time. The rock that struck the statue grew into a huge mountain that filled the whole earth. After he had reminded the king what the dream was, Daniel explained it, showing what was to come.

The Kingdoms of This World

According to Daniel's explanation, the gold head stood for Nebuchadnezzar himself. Daniel said, "You, O king, are the king of kings. The God of heaven has given you dominion and power and might and glory; in your hands he has placed mankind and the beasts of the field and the birds of the air. Wherever they live, he has made you ruler over them all. You are that head of gold" (vv. 37–38).

This brief description of the importance of Babylon in world history is surprisingly accurate. It is significant that this is the point at which the vision starts. One reason is that Nebuchadnezzar was then living and Babylon was the world empire of the time. But in the biblical perspective Babylon is also the first and prototype of all world empires. The Bible introduces Babylon in the early chapters of Genesis as the center of Nimrod's empire (Gen. 10:8–12), the place where men first banded together against God, who scattered them by the confusion of their language (Gen. 11:1–9). Apparently Babylon had always been great, but it had risen to heights of previously unmatched magnificence under Nebuchadnezzar. It was there, for example, that the famous "hanging gardens," one of the wonders of the ancient world, were located.

But this was God's doing, not Nebuchadnezzar's. Notice the dominant position given to God in these sentences: "*The God of heaven* has given you dominion and power and might and glory"; "in your hands *he* has placed mankind and the beasts of the field and the birds of the air"; "*he* has made you ruler over them all" (Dan. 2:37–38). Nebuchadnezzar will dispute this, which is what the third and fourth chapters of Daniel are about. But he is to learn that it is God nevertheless who has set him up and that it is God who will also take him down. As Nebuchadnezzar later acknowledges, "[God] does as he pleases with the powers of heaven and the peoples of the earth" (Dan. 4:35).

The second part of the statue was the silver part, representing a kingdom that would succeed but would be inferior to that of Nebuchadnezzar. In the unfolding of history this became the kingdom of the Medes and Persians, brought to its zenith of power by King Darius. Darius is introduced to us at the end of Daniel 5.

The third part of the statue was made of brass. It represented the kingdom of the Greeks established by Alexander the Great. Alexander was a remarkable man and a military genius. He was born in Macedonia. But after the death of his father, Philip, in 336 B.C., he crossed the Hellespont into what we call Turkey, at that time a portion of the Persian Empire. His first victory was at Granicus, where he defeated the armies of the frontier governors. Later he overwhelmed the armies of Darius III at the decisive battle of Issus in 333 B.C. He marched south against the kingdoms of the eastern Mediterranean and eventually moved east as far as the Indus River, where, so the story goes, he wept because he had no more worlds to conquer.

The fourth part of the statue, the part made of iron and the feet made of iron mixed with baked clay, represented the Roman Empire. Although this kingdom was still hundreds of years in the future as Daniel spoke, Daniel nevertheless described it accurately. "There will be a fourth kingdom, strong as iron—for iron breaks and smashes everything—and as iron breaks things to pieces, so it will crush and break all the others. Just as you saw that the feet and toes were partly of baked clay and partly of iron, so this will be a divided kingdom; yet it will have some of the strength of iron in it, even as you saw iron mixed with clay. As the toes were partly iron and partly clay, so this kingdom will be partly strong and partly brittle. And just as you saw the iron mixed with baked clay, so the people will be a mixture and will not remain united, any more than iron mixes with clay" (Dan. 2:40–43).

This is most remarkable! As I said earlier, this accurate forecast of the gentile world empires following the fall of Babylon is the chief reason why liberal scholars of the past tried so hard to discredit this book, assigning it to a later era. But even with such late datings, Daniel still precedes some of the events it prophesies by hundreds of years. Such prophecies are one proof of the Bible's divine inspiration.[1]

But they are also proof of God's sovereignty, which is the dominant theme in Daniel. How so? It is because the only way in which God can foretell what is going to come about in history is if God is in control of history. He is able to foretell what will happen because he has determined what will happen and because he has the power to make it happen. What is more, this shows God to be the true God.

God presents this argument in Isaiah 41. There God challenges the false gods of the time by asking them to tell the future as proof that they are real gods. Or failing that, he challenges them to do something—anything—to show their value.

> "Present your case," says the LORD.
>   "Set forth your arguments," says Jacob's King.
> "Bring in your idols to tell us
>   what is going to happen.
> Tell us what the former things were,
>   so that we may consider them
>   and know their final outcome.
> Or declare to us the things to come,
>   tell us what the future holds,
>   so we may know that you are gods.
> Do something, whether good or bad,
>   so that we will be dismayed and filled with fear.
> But you are less than nothing
>   and your works are utterly worthless;
>   he who chooses you is detestable."
>
>   Isaiah 41:21–24

Sometimes fortune-tellers make shrewd guesses about some future happening—if it is not too far in the future. The devil, if he speaks through fortune-tellers, mediums, and mystics, can no doubt be even shrewder than that. But nowhere in all history is there a rival to the distant, detailed, and yet accurately fulfilled prophecies of the biblical writers. This is one strong proof of the Bible's inspiration and of the identification of the God of the Bible as the true God.

Pomp of Yesterday

There is another thing to be seen about Daniel's prophecy concerning this world's empires before we consider the great stone that is the climax of the vision. It is the decline of glory and even the decline of power that this vision represents.

Daniel makes the point explicitly, showing that each kingdom is "inferior" to the one before it in terms of its glory. That is to say, gold is the most precious of metals, and since the golden head of the statue represents Babylon, Babylon was therefore the most glorious of the four world kingdoms. Silver is less precious than gold, therefore less glorious. Brass is less precious than silver, therefore also a step further down in splendor. Iron, the basest of these metals, is the least glorious of all. Yet each of these is also stronger up to a point. Silver is stronger than gold. Brass is stronger than silver. Iron is stronger than brass. Daniel stresses this, saying, "Iron breaks and smashes everything." The kingdoms of the world seem to be trading magnificence for strength, which they must do if the succeeding empires are each to be sufficiently strong to destroy their predecessors. Yet, strikingly, when the vision gets to the strongest empire of all, the Roman Empire, the dream shows that the kingdom is (or would be) divided and in its divided state would have its strength, iron, mixed with brittle clay.

This is the opposite of the humanistic view of world progress. In its purest form the doctrine of progress insists that progress must always occur on all fronts. This is not true, of course. There are declines as well as gains. So modified expressions of the "progress" philosophy argue that losses in one area (glory or magnificence, for example) are more than compensated for by gains in another area (strength or power, to preserve the example). But even that is an illusion, according to this chapter. When we go on with God, as Daniel and his friends did go on, we move on from strength to strength, from victory to victory. This is real progress, both personal and social. But apart from God even our imagined advances are declines.

Is the United States not morally and spiritually weaker today, though physically stronger, than it was a generation ago? Is not the same thing true for most other technically advanced societies?

The Stone the Builders Rejected

We come, then, to the climax of the king's dream: the rock that struck the feet of the statue, destroyed it, and then grew to be a mountain that filled the whole earth. Daniel interpreted this part of the dream, saying, "In the time of those kings, the God of heaven will set up a kingdom that will never be destroyed, nor will it be left to another people. It will crush all those kingdoms and bring them to an end, but it will itself endure forever. This is the meaning of the vision of the rock cut out of a mountain, but not by human hands—a rock that broke the iron, the bronze, the clay, the silver and the gold to pieces" (Dan. 2:44–45).

Understanding this is both easy and hard. The easy part is the identification of the rock with Jesus Christ. To begin with, mention of the rock unveils a rich lode of biblical imagery. The first and germinal reference is Psalm 118:22: "The stone the builders rejected has become the capstone."

This refers to something that happened in the building of Solomon's temple in Jerusalem. The stones for the temple were quarried far from the temple site, according to detailed plans supplied by the temple architects, and they were transported to the site and assembled without the noise of stone-cutting tools. Early in the construction a stone was sent that did not seem to fit. Since the builders did not know what to do with it, they laid it aside and forgot it. Later when they came to place a large capstone on their now nearly completed structure and sent to the quarry for it, they were told that it was not there, that it had already been sent up. They searched for it, found the stone that had been laid aside earlier, and installed it. It fit perfectly. Thus, "the stone the builders rejected [became] the capstone."

Jesus applied this and the following verse to himself, saying,

Have you never read in the Scriptures:

> "The stone the builders rejected
>   has become the capstone;
> the Lord has done this,
>   and it is marvelous in our eyes"?

Therefore I tell you that the kingdom of God will be taken away from you and given to a people who will produce its fruit. He who falls on this stone will be broken to pieces, but he on whom it falls will be crushed.

Matthew 21:42–44

Isaiah 28:16 is another well-known text based on this image.

> See, I lay a stone in Zion,
>   a tested stone,
> a precious cornerstone for a sure foundation;
>   the one who trusts will never be dismayed.

In the New Testament, Peter quotes both those passages in reference to Jesus, adding in the third place Isaiah 8:14 for good measure.

Scripture . . . says,

> "See, I lay a stone in Zion,
>   a chosen and precious cornerstone,
> and the one who trusts in him
>   will never be put to shame."

Now to you who believe, this stone is precious. But to those who do not believe,

> "The stone the builders rejected
>   has become the capstone,"

and,

> "A stone that causes men to stumble
>   and a rock that makes them fall"

1 Peter 2:6–8

These passages (and others) make clear that the rock of Nebuchadnezzar's dream is Jesus Christ—a divine Christ, "not [made] by human hands"—and the mountain of the dream is his kingdom. That is the easy part of the interpretation.

The difficult part has to do with the place in human history where that great kingdom is to be located. Is it in the present, here and now? Does it refer to the church and its expansion throughout the world? The church's destruction of the world's kingdoms? That is one explanation. Or does it refer to the kingdom of Christ still to come? That is the second explanation. As is often the case with interpretation like this, there are pros and cons on both sides.

The great strength of the view that the church is the rock that grows up to be a mountain that fills the whole earth is the historical sequence. If the parts of the statue represent the kingdoms of Babylon, Persia, Greece, and Rome, as I have indicated, it is hard to escape noticing that Jesus came to earth in the days of the Roman Empire and that his church has gradually expanded into all corners of the world from that time to this. Moreover, we have Christ's significant words to Peter: "You are Peter, and on this rock I will build my church, and the gates of Hades will not overcome it" (Matt. 16:18). Most (but not all) in the Reformed camp hold to this position.

Unfortunately, the matter is not so simple as this argument suggests. The dream given to Nebuchadnezzar suggests that the fourth empire, Rome, would be divided into two parts (the legs) and then into ten affiliated but separate kingdoms (the toes). This happened. The empire divided into two parts, its eastern and western halves, and later it disintegrated even further. But this happened *after* the birth of Christ, not before, which is what the dream requires. Again, although it is true that the church of Christ has expanded to fill the whole world in some sense, it has not destroyed the world's kingdoms, which is what the dream demands. The empires of the world have not fallen; they have not broken into pieces and been scattered like chaff. In other words, there has been no great catastrophe from the world's perspective.

On the other side of the argument, the view that sees the rock that fills the earth as a future ("millennial") reign of Christ can insist on the catastrophic aspect. Indeed, it is suggested by later books of prophecy, especially Revelation, which portrays a sudden return of Christ, a millennium, and a final judgment. If Christ is actually to rule on earth, establishing an earthly and not merely a spiritual kingdom, then other kingdoms obviously must be overthrown, and it is easy to imagine the overthrow of ten independent but confederated kingdoms.

The weakness of this view is that Nebuchadnezzar's dream fails to account for the intervening years of church expansion. Adherents must speak of a "gap" in prophecy into which the "times of the Gentiles" fit. Some have said that prophecy *per se* relates almost exclusively to Israel and that there is therefore something like a stopping of the "prophetic clock" until the times of the Gentiles are fulfilled.[2] This is the dominant view of dispensationalists and of most writers of prophecy in the last generation.

Kiss the Son

In my opinion, the second of these views, the view of the dispensationalists, is the best interpretation of Daniel 2—though I am not a dispensationalist. But I want to emphasize that the main point made by Daniel's interpretation of this dream is not the precise period of history in which the kingdom of Christ will grow and fill the earth, or how that will happen, but rather that it *will* happen and that the kingdoms of this world will be scattered before it. Daniel's real point is that of Psalm 2.

In Psalm 2 we are told how the kings and people of the earth take their stand against the Lord and his Anointed, saying, "Let us break their chains . . . and throw off their fetters" (v. 3). But what is the reaction of God to this act of cosmic arrogance? Does God tremble before kings like Nebuchadnezzar or the secularists of our time? Not at all! The psalm says that God laughs at their rebellion. This is the only place in the entire Bible where we are told that God laughs, and it is not a good-humored, mirthful laugh. It is a laugh of derision.

> The One enthroned in heaven laughs;
>   the Lord scoffs at them.
> Then he rebukes them in his anger
>   and terrifies them in his wrath, saying,
> "I have installed my King
>   on Zion, my holy hill."
>
>   verses 4–6

That is Daniel's chief message for Nebuchadnezzar and for our own time. The kingdoms of this world are powerful and sometimes even glorious—from our point of view. But even their strength is given to them by God, and just as God sets up kingdoms, so does he bring them down and dispose of them. He was to do that with Nebuchadnezzar. He has done that with all the world's past kingdoms, and he will do it with those of our time.

For our part, the only wise course is to recognize that "the kingdom of the world has become the kingdom of our Lord and of his Christ" (Rev. 11:15) and to "kiss the Son" in grateful devotion.

5

Faith in the Furnace

Daniel 3:1–30

Shadrach, Meshach and Abednego replied to the king, "O Nebuchadnezzar, we do not need to defend ourselves before you in this matter. If we are thrown into the blazing furnace, the God we serve is able to save us from it, and he will rescue us from your hand, O king. But even if he does not, we want you to know, O king, that we will not serve your gods or worship the image of gold you have set up."

When I was a student at Harvard University, I worked as an engineer in the college radio station. One day we were recording some dramatic Bible readings, and the man being recorded was a Jewish drama student who later established a repertory company in Boston. We came to Daniel 3, which in his judgment was comedy and to be handled as such. He began to read from an older version of the Bible the lists of Babylonian officials ("the princes, the governors, and the captains, the judges, the treasurers, the counsellors, the sheriffs" [v. 3 KJV]) and instruments ("cornet, flute, harp, sackbutt, psaltery, dulcimer" [v. 5 KJV]) as if this were one of the most humorous things in the world.

I was offended by this reading. So although it was not my job to interfere with what was being done in the studio, I interrupted to say that this was an injustice to one of the great stories of the world and that in addition it was disrespectful to the Word of God.

My interruptions shocked the drama student—largely, I suppose, because a Gentile was objecting to a reading of what he considered to be his book particularly. So although I expected a quick rebuff or insult, he actually listened as I explained the story of how these three brave Jewish men risked their lives for the sake of their loyalty to God. After that the man I was recording settled down and handled the story with much more respect, and from that time on (if not before) the story of Shadrach, Meshach, and Abednego became one of my favorite stories in the Bible.

Nebuchadnezzar's Gold Image

The narrative begins with a plan conceived by Nebuchadnezzar. Nebuchadnezzar built a great golden statue, which he set up on the plain of Dura. It was made of gold, and it was ninety feet high and nine feet wide. Ninety feet is twice as high as most row houses in Philadelphia, so this was a gigantic statue that must have required enormous amounts of gold. Even if the statue was only covered with gold, it still would have taken a great amount. But this is what he did, and the fact that the statue was of gold is the thing of chief importance.

In order to understand the reason for Nebuchadnezzar's building this statue, we have to go back to the previous chapter in which he had dreamed of a statue, the head of which was of gold, the breast and arms of silver, the middle portion of bronze, the legs of iron, and the feet and toes of iron mixed with baked clay. As Daniel interpreted the dream, the head represented the glorious kingdom of Babylon, the silver a less glorious but stronger kingdom (that of the Medes and Persians) that would follow Nebuchadnezzar's, the brass a still less glorious but stronger kingdom (that of the Greeks), and the iron the strongest but basest kingdom of all (that of Rome). At the end of this history, a rock, representing Christ, would strike the world's kingdoms, destroy them, and then grow to fill the whole earth.

As we read this interpretation it does not seem to be at all threatening. Kingdoms do succeed other kingdoms, and (we believe) the kingdom of Christ will surpass them all.

But this is not the way Nebuchadnezzar must have seen it. After Daniel had revealed the dream and its meaning to Nebuchadnezzar, Nebuchadnezzar praised Daniel's God, saying, "Surely your God is the God of gods and the Lord of kings and a revealer of mysteries, for you were able to reveal this mystery" (Dan. 2:47). But when he got to thinking about it later, Nebuchadnezzar was not at all pleased. He must have said to himself, "Wouldn't it be nice if more of that statue were gold than just the head? The head represents me, and I'm glad that I'm the head and not a toe, for example. But it would really be nice if I were not just the head but the whole statue. Why should my kingdom be succeeded by other kingdoms? Why shouldn't this great Babylon that I have built last forever?" So Nebuchadnezzar built a statue that represented his will for the future. It was *all* of gold. In this way he defied God and said in effect, "I will not allow the God of Daniel to set my kingdom aside. My rule will endure."

At this point we begin to understand why this is not a humorous story and why it is actually another chapter in what we have already seen to be the theme of this book: Whose god is God? Who rules history? It is why this matter of bowing down to the statue was more than just a question of bowing down or not bowing down to an idol—though it certainly was that. It was a matter of bowing before the will or rebelling against the will of God.

Shadrach, Meshach, and Abednego

Daniel does not appear in this incident. We do not know why. The construction of Nebuchadnezzar's gold statue seems to have happened early in his career, when he was still young. So it is probable that he had been assigned work in some other portion of the empire. At any rate, he does not seem to have been in Babylon at this time, and the storm broke instead on Shadrach, Meshach, and Abednego, his three friends.

The trouble began with the Chaldeans, or astrologers, for whose work the four young Jews had been trained. They told the king that Shadrach, Meshach, and Abednego were defying the decree that whenever the horn, flute, zither, lyre, harp, pipes, and other instruments sounded, everyone was to fall down and worship the great golden image. "There are some Jews whom you have set over the affairs of the province of Babylon—Shadrach, Meshach and Abednego—who pay no attention to you, O king. They neither serve your gods nor worship the image of gold you have set up" (Dan. 3:12).

Why did they say this? Why did they accuse these from among their own number? I think it is not at all hard to discover the reason for their actions as jealousy and resentment toward those who had been part of the interpretation of Nebuchadnezzar's earlier dream, which they themselves had been unable to discern. It was the same motivation that causes coworkers to slander or gossip about each other when they should be building one another up. It is the thing that causes unpleasantness in schools or sibling rivalry.

The convictions of Shadrach, Meshach, and Abednego provided their enemy coworkers with an opportunity to accuse them of treason, and this is what they did, phrasing their remarks in such a manner as to work Nebuchadnezzar into the greatest possible agitation. Furious with rage, Nebuchadnezzar brought the three young men before him and probed for a confession in the case. "Is it true, Shadrach, Meshach and Abednego, that you do not serve my gods or worship the image of gold I have set up?" (v. 14).

No reply is recorded, but there must have been one. They must have told the king that what he had been told about them was correct.

Nebuchadnezzar offered to give them another chance. "Now when you hear the sound of the horn, flute, zither, lyre, harp, pipes and all kinds of music, if you are ready to fall down and worship the image I made, very good. But if you do not worship it, you will be thrown immediately into a blazing furnace. Then what god will be able to rescue you from my hand?" (v. 15). That was the situation, the ultimatum imposed upon the three men.

Let me say at this point—so that we will understand this story at the proper level—that this is the problem that confronts every follower of the true God when the requirements of serving him come into conflict with the demands of a secular state. I mean by this not merely a demand to do an openly wicked thing or die for refusing to do it (like refusing to turn over or kill Jews in Nazi Germany). I mean any pressure to disobey the teachings of the Bible, whether by peers in your school, by fellow employees, by employers, or by whoever it may be. Whenever you are pressured to do something (or not to do something) that you know by the teachings of the Bible to be wrong (or right), your situation is that of these three men and your responsibility before God is the same also. You must do the right. You must not bow to the world's demands, even if the consequences are costly.

You say, "But we are commanded to obey the state."

Yes, in all areas of its legitimate authority. Paul wrote, "Give everyone what you owe him: If you owe taxes, pay taxes; if revenue, then revenue; if respect, then respect; if honor, then honor" (Rom. 13:7). Moreover, in obeying the state we must know that God has established such authorities (Rom. 13:1–5). Daniel and his friends knew this—at least after the interpretation of Nebuchadnezzar's dream, if not before. God had established Nebuchadnezzar. He had made him to be the head of gold. But notice: the fact that Nebuchadnezzar had been established by God did not make Nebuchadnezzar God. The fact that God raises up rulers does not make rulers autonomous. It does not give them unlimited power. On the contrary, it limits their power, for they are responsible to the One who has set them up—whether they acknowledge him as God or not. The duty of believers is to remind the state of this divine limitation. They are to do it by words and, if necessary, by the laying down of their lives.

The Sovereign God

When the ultimatum was put to these three men, we do not read that they took time to think the issues through. Even the great Martin Luther asked for a night to pray and think when he was asked to recant. But Shadrach, Meshach, and Abednego seem to have responded at once: "O Nebuchadnezzar, we do not need to defend ourselves before you in this matter. If we are thrown into the blazing furnace, the God we serve is able to save us from it, and he will rescue us from your hand, O king. But even if he does not, we want you to know, O king, that we will not serve your gods or worship the image of gold you have set up" (Dan. 3:16–18).

There are times in life when you do not want to debate the pros and cons of a position. If you do, you will very likely choose the wrong side. There are times when you have to respond the right way and do the right thing instantly, or you will probably fail the test.

What if Shadrach, Meshach, and Abednego had listened to our kinds of rationalizations? Someone might have said, "The three of you are obviously sincere and quite dedicated. We need more people like you, and that is just the reason why you must listen to reason in this matter. Because if you do not listen and instead persist in this obstinate disobedience, you are going to be killed and your beneficial influence on Babylon will be over. Consider first that your disobedience is already being entirely misunderstood. You think that you are standing for the identity of the true God. But what you are doing is actually being construed as political rebellion, defiance of the king's order. You are not going to be executed for religion but for civil disobedience. So what good does persisting in this rebellious state do? The proper course is to bow down, live, and extend your 'godly' influence in other ways."

Or again, a wise head might have argued, "Understand that Nebuchadnezzar is actually on your side. He did not need to give you a hearing. When he did, he did not need to give you another chance. He has done these things only because he is already well-disposed toward you and likes you. He does not want to execute you. I think that if you would only stand at a distance from the statue and tip your head forward slightly—you won't need to prostrate yourselves on the ground—Nebuchadnezzar would be pleased by that and respect you all the more. He would realize that it was a difficult thing for you to do, but that you did it for his sake. It takes men of courage to compromise like that."

A theologian might have gotten into the argument. "Remember that in the New Testament it says—I know the New Testament hasn't been written yet, but it will be—'an idol is nothing.' Now if 'an idol is nothing,' then to fall down and worship Nebuchadnezzar's golden image is to fall down and worship nothing, and worshiping nothing cannot possibly be construed as idolatry, can it?"

If Shadrach, Meshach, and Abednego had stopped to consider these arguments, they might have wavered. But they did not stop to consider them or waver because they already knew where they stood and why they stood there. In other words, they had already wrestled through such issues and knew that whatever else they might have been, they were first and foremost worshipers of the true God, and he had said, "You shall have no other gods before me. You shall not make for yourself an idol in the form of anything in heaven above or on the earth beneath or in the waters below. You shall not bow down to them or worship them; for I, the LORD your God, am a jealous God, punishing the children for the sin of the fathers to the third and fourth generation of those who hate me, but showing love to a thousand generations of those who love me and keep my commandments" (Exod. 20:3–6).

There were three things that gave Shadrach, Meshach, and Abednego the strength to stand firm in this great test of their commitment.

1. *They knew that God was sovereign.* Nothing is clearer in their response to King Nebuchadnezzar than this: "The God we serve *is able* to save us," and if he chooses to do so, "*he will* rescue us from your hand, O king." This is no

airy, speculative abstraction. This is faith in the furnace. It is a firm conviction of the sovereignty of God in the midst of all things contrary. These men knew that God is sovereign, and therefore it was not foolish but wise for them to entrust their lives to him in this matter.

2. *They knew the Scriptures.* This is the reason they refused to bow down: God had forbidden it. But knowing the Scriptures is also important for the reason that moral issues seldom come to us in black-and-white terms. The world makes moral issues as ambiguous as possible, because when that is the case, it seems to free us to do what we want to do—or at least to do what we judge best in the circumstances. If we are to do the right thing in such circumstances, we must know the Word of God, because only the Word of God will cut through such ambiguity. Shadrach, Meshach, and Abednego triumphed because their minds were filled with Scripture and because they kept coming back to Scripture as the only fully trustworthy and inerrant authority in all matters.

3. *They were willing to die for their convictions.* I am sure you can see why this is important. It is important because it is possible to believe in a sovereign God and know from Scripture what that sovereign God requires and yet fail to do the right thing because you are unwilling to pay the price of obedience. It is true that not many of us are likely to be faced with a choice between compromise or execution. I hope you never will be. But the issue is the same regardless of the penalty. Many fail because they will not pay the price of a loss of popularity or loneliness or ridicule or persecution or economic hardship. Only those who are willing to pay such prices make a difference.

I think of Dr. Joseph Tson, the Romanian pastor who before his exile was called before the Communist authorities to answer for his religious convictions and preaching. He expected to be killed. So he set his affairs in order, and when he appeared before the interrogating officer, he said, "I have to tell you first that I am ready to die. I have put my affairs in order. Your supreme weapon is killing. My supreme weapon is dying, because when you kill me people all over Romania will read my books and believe on the God I preach—even more than they do now."

The interrogator replied, "Who said anything about killing?" and eventually let him go. Today Joseph Tson is in America, where he prepares weekly radio broadcasts into Romania that are listened to by most of the population. He is heard because he would rather have died than compromise.

Through the Deep Waters

Some people do pay for their faith by dying, of course. But in other cases, like that of Joseph Tson, God intervenes to spare his servants. He spared Shadrach, Meshach, and Abednego. You know the story. Nebuchadnezzar was furious that the three young Jews would not obey him, so he ordered the furnace heated seven times hotter than usual—in case the Jewish God was able to save from normally heated furnaces only—and had Shadrach,

Meshach, and Abednego thrown into it. The flames from the superheated furnace killed the men who took the three Jews to it, but Shadrach, Meshach, and Abednego were not killed. Instead, when Nebuchadnezzar peered into the furnace, he saw them walking around in the fire, unbound and unharmed. And he also saw a fourth person who looked "like a son of the gods" (Dan. 3:25).

It is not difficult to know who that fourth person was. He was Jesus Christ in a preincarnate form—perhaps the form he had when he appeared to Abraham before the destruction of Sodom and Gomorrah or in which he wrestled with Jacob beside the brook Jabbok. It is a vivid portrayal of the fact that God stands with his people in their troubles. We sing in one of our hymns:

> When through the deep waters I call thee to go,
> The rivers of woe shall not thee overflow;
> For I will be with thee thy troubles to bless,
> And sanctify to thee thy deepest distress.
>
> When through fiery trials thy pathway shall lie,
> My grace, all sufficient, shall be thy supply;
> The flame shall not hurt thee; I only design
> Thy dross to consume, and thy gold to refine.

God does go with his people in their trials. Countless believers have testified to that. So let us be confident in the promise of that presence and be strong. Let us stand for the right and do it. Let us refuse to compromise. Let us stand with unbowed heads and rigid backbones before the golden statues of our godless, materialistic culture. Let us declare that there is a God to be served and a race to be won. Let us shout that we are determined to receive God's prize, which is far greater than this world's tinsel toys, and that we are servants of him before whom every knee will bow.

What of Nebuchadnezzar? He was impressed. He said, "Praise be to the God of Shadrach, Meshach and Abednego, who has sent his angel and rescued his servants! They trusted in him and defied the king's command and were willing to give up their lives rather than serve or worship any god except their own God. Therefore I decree that the people of any nation or language who say anything against the God of Shadrach, Meshach and Abednego be cut into pieces and their houses be turned into piles of rubble, for no other god can save in this way" (vv. 28–29). But Nebuchadnezzar was not converted. He was going to have to sink much lower before he was ready to acknowledge that there is but one God and to worship him.

6

The Sin God Will Not Tolerate

Daniel 4:1-37

Twelve months later, as the king was walking on the roof of the royal palace of Babylon, he said, "Is not this the great Babylon I have built as the royal residence, by my mighty power and for the glory of my majesty?"

The words were still on his lips when a voice came from heaven, "This is what is decreed for you, King Nebuchadnezzar: Your royal authority has been taken from you. You will be driven away from people and will live with the wild animals; you will eat grass like cattle. Seven times will pass by for you until you acknowledge that the Most High is sovereign over the kingdoms of men and gives them to anyone he wishes."

Immediately what had been said about Nebuchadnezzar was fulfilled. He was driven away from people and ate grass like cattle. His body was drenched with the dew of heaven until his hair grew like the feathers of an eagle and his nails like the claws of a bird.

At the end of that time, I, Nebuchadnezzar, raised my eyes toward heaven, and my sanity was restored. Then I praised the Most High; I honored and glorified him who lives forever.

I have entitled this study "The Sin God Will Not Tolerate," but I am sure you understand that in the ultimate sense there is no sin God will tolerate. All sin will be judged. Many sins are judged in this life; all sins will be judged in the life to come. Thus in using this title I am speaking in a different sense, and what I want to point out is that although God does temporarily tolerate some sins in this world, yet there is one sin that God does not seem

48

to countenance. Daniel 4, which concludes the story of Nebuchadnezzar, deals with this matter.

Background to the Story

The key to understanding these early chapters, and perhaps the entire Book of Daniel, comes in the second verse of the book, as I explained earlier. That verse tells of the conquest of Jerusalem by Nebuchadnezzar and explains that after the conquest of the city, Nebuchadnezzar brought back the vessels of the temple of God in Jerusalem to the house of his god and laid them up in the treasure house of his god. By this symbolic act Nebuchadnezzar was asserting that his gods were stronger than Jehovah. And so it seemed. We know that God permits others to triumph over his people for his own reasons, generally to bring judgment for sin. The temporary victory of evil persons does not mean that God is not more powerful than evil or that he will not ultimately be victorious. Yet this is what Nebuchadnezzar thought. These opening chapters of Daniel show Jehovah teaching this proud monarch that neither his gods nor Nebuchadnezzar himself was stronger than the Most High. God is God! "My glory I will not give to another," says God. He does not allow Nebuchadnezzar to give God's glory to another in this story.

God had already been trying to teach Nebuchadnezzar that. The first story in Daniel that really involves Nebuchadnezzar is the story of the dream he had of a great image. It was a figure of gold, silver, brass, and iron. Nebuchadnezzar was represented by the gold head of the image. This was God's acknowledgment that his kingdom was indeed magnificent but that, as God pointed out, it would be succeeded by another (as all human kingdoms are) and that by another and that by another; and only at the end would come the eternal kingdom of God in Christ. This kingdom would overthrow all others, grow up, and fill the earth. God was teaching Nebuchadnezzar that he was not so important as he thought.

The next story in Daniel concerns the gold image that Nebuchadnezzar set up in the plain of Dura. In reading the story with Nebuchadnezzar's vision in view, we realize that Nebuchadnezzar was rebelling against God's decree. God had said, "Your kingdom will be succeeded by other kingdoms, kingdoms of silver, brass, and iron." Nebuchadnezzar replied, "No, my kingdom will endure forever; it will always be glorious. Therefore, I will create a statue of which not only the head will be gold, but also the thighs and legs and feet. All of it will be gold. That is going to represent me and my descendants forever." Now God has to humble Nebuchadnezzar and show that only God is King.

"Babylon, That I Have Built"

The story we have in Daniel 4 has to do with another vision, but it must be seen against this background. Nebuchadnezzar dreamed again, and this time he dreamed that he saw a great tree. The details of this dream are so interesting that I cite it in full. Nebuchadnezzar is speaking.

> These are the visions I saw while lying in my bed: I looked, and there before me stood a tree in the middle of the land. Its height was enormous. The tree grew large and strong and its top touched the sky; it was visible to the ends of the earth. Its leaves were beautiful, its fruit abundant, and on it was food for all. Under it the beasts of the field found shelter, and the birds of the air lived in its branches; from it every creature was fed.
>
> In the visions I saw while lying in my bed, I looked, and there before me was a messenger, a holy one, coming down from heaven. He called in a loud voice: "Cut down the tree and trim off its branches; strip off its leaves and scatter its fruit. Let the animals flee from under it and the birds from its branches. But let the stump and its roots, bound with iron and bronze, remain in the ground, in the grass of the field.
>
> "Let him be drenched with the dew of heaven, and let him live with the animals among the plants of the earth. Let his mind be changed from that of a man and let him be given the mind of an animal, till seven times pass by for him.
>
> "The decision is announced by messengers; the holy ones declare the verdict, so that the living may know that the Most High is sovereign over the kingdoms of men and gives them to anyone he wishes and sets over them the lowliest of men."

verses 10–17

After receiving this vision Nebuchadnezzar consulted the Chaldeans as he had done on other occasions, but they were unable to give the meaning. Eventually he turned to Daniel, who apparently understood it at once. Daniel saw that the vision referred to the king. So we read that his countenance was troubled for about an hour, bothered, obviously, by what he knew this meant. Finally Nebuchadnezzar said, "Don't be bothered. I understand that this is not a good vision, but tell me about it anyway. I want to know the truth."

Daniel began to explain the vision. He explained that the tree was Nebuchadnezzar. God had exalted him to be a great figure, to fill all the world with his empire. Those of the earth were nourished by him—the birds in the branches, the beasts under the tree—all were fed. But because his heart was lifted up through pride, God was going to cause this great tree to be cut down. He was not to die. But he was going to lose his sanity for seven years until he came to recognize that the Most High God rules in the affairs of men. This God sets up whom he will and brings down whom he will, and when he sets a man up, he can do it from the basest of men. He does not have to choose what we would regard as the best.

The story goes on to show that this is precisely what happened. The time came when Nebuchadnezzar was walking in his palace, looking out over the great city of Babylon, and he took to himself the glory that he should have given God. He said, "Look at this great Babylon that I have built." In the same hour the prophecy took place. Nebuchadnezzar's mind went from him, and he was driven from the palace into the fields, in the way, presumably, that they treated the insane in those days. Thus he made his home with the beasts. His fingernails grew long like claws, and his hair became matted; he was unable to take care of himself. At the end of the time, his reason returned to him—we are to understand that this was not only in a mental sense but also in a spiritual sense—and he recognized the truth of things, coming to what we would call a genuine repentance. We find his words of repentance and praise for God at the end of the chapter.

Verse 30 is the key. It contains Nebuchadnezzar's boast. What Nebuchadnezzar says as he looks out over mighty Babylon is: "Is not this the great Babylon I have built as the royal residence, by my mighty power and for the glory of my majesty?" He said, "Look what *I* have done!" He failed to give God the glory. That verse is the expression of Nebuchadnezzar's heart and of our hearts apart from the grace of God. We think that we are responsible for what we do and achieve, and we do not recognize that even when we achieve great things it is because God, the giver of all good gifts, has given us the ability to achieve them.

The Most High God

Lay that perspective over against the unique name for God that we find six times in this chapter but which has never occurred in the Book of Daniel before this point. The name is "the Most High." You find it in a slightly different form in verse 2: "the Most High God." Then you find it exactly in verses 17, 24, 25, 32, and 34.

What does this name signify? Well, if you get out a concordance and look to see where else it occurs in the Old Testament, you will find that the first time the name appears is in Genesis in connection with the story of Abraham's return from the battle against the kings and his meeting with Melchizedek. We are told there that Melchizedek was the priest of the Most High God, ruler of heaven and earth. That phrase explains the name. It is not referring to God's role as Redeemer or to his wisdom. It relates to God's sovereignty. "The Most High God" is the God who rules, not only in heaven but on earth.

A bit further on in the Old Testament, in Isaiah 14, we have a description of the thoughts that went through the mind of Satan in the moment of his rebellion against God. One of the things Satan said is that he wished to be like the Most High. He said, "I will ascend to heaven; I will raise my throne above the stars of God; I will sit enthroned on the mount of assembly, on the utmost heights of the sacred mountain. I will ascend above the tops of the clouds: I will make myself like the Most High" (vv. 13–14).

Why did Satan not say, "I will be like the Redeemer"? Why did he not say, "I will be like the most wise God"? Why not one of God's other names? It is because he was not interested in those aspects of God's character. He wanted to be like God in his sovereign rule. In other words, he said, "I am going to take God down from his throne and put myself upon the throne, and I am going to rule in God's place."

That is the meaning of "the Most High." And here is Nebuchadnezzar saying, with all the folly of which human beings are capable, "Look at this great Babylon that *I*, Nebuchadnezzar, have built." God replied, "That is the sin I will not tolerate," and he brings him down.

Of course, this is not just Satan's sin. This is not just Nebuchadnezzar's sin. This is our sin, and it is ours both individually and collectively as a nation. The greatest sin of all is that we take glory to ourselves instead of giving credit to God. When we do well we think it is our achievement. When we do badly we think it is somebody else's fault. It is the perspective of fallen humanity, and what we do as individuals in the leading of our daily lives we do nationally. America has known real greatness. It has been greatly blessed financially, culturally, spiritually, and in many other ways. But instead of giving glory to God, from whom such blessing comes, we boast of our achievement, assuming that it is because we are the kind of people we intrinsically are.

God says, "I will not tolerate that, in either individuals or nations." The history of humanity is (1) the raising up of a nation by the blessing of God, (2) men and women taking glory to themselves, and (3) God tearing them down in order to show that he is the Most High God and not mankind. That will happen in America. I believe it is happening already. It will happen to a greater extent unless we repent.

Bestial Behavior

The next part of the story is about Nebuchadnezzar's punishment, and it is significant. It is not a case of God merely going down a list of the various punishments available and saying, "Let's see now . . . Nebuchadnezzar. Eeny, meeny, miney, moe—let's take this one: *insanity*." God does not operate that way. Everything God does is significant. So when God caused Nebuchadnezzar to be lowered from the pinnacle of pride to the baseness of insanity and to be associated with the beasts and behave like a beast, God was saying by that punishment that this is the result when men give the glory of God to themselves. They become beastlike. In fact, they become even worse than beasts. Because beasts, when they are beastlike, are at least behaving the way beasts should behave. But we, when we become beastlike, behave not only like beasts, which is below where we should behave and is therefore bad enough, but even worse than beasts.

John Gerstner, a frequent speaker at the Philadelphia Conference on Reformed Theology, was teaching on one occasion about the depravity of man and compared men and women to rats. After he had finished his address, there was a question-and-answer period, and somebody who was greatly offended by the comparison stood up and asked him to apologize. The questioner said it was "insulting" to compare men and women to rats. Dr. Gerstner apologized. "I do apologize," he said. "I apologize profusely. The comparison was terribly unfair . . . to the rats." He then went on to show that what a rat does, it does by the gifts of God that make it ratlike. But when we behave like rats, we behave worse than we should and even worse than rats.

Let me show what happens when men and women take the glory of God to themselves. You have it in Romans 1, where God says he gives men up. When he gives them up, he does not give them up to nothing. Rather, he gives them up to the working out of the moral laws of the universe that he has established, and these laws decree that if you will not have God and therefore will not have truth, holiness, justice, righteousness, and all the other good gifts that have come from him, you will inevitably have the opposite. The first chapter of Romans shows that when men turned from God, God turned from men and they inevitably went downhill.

God gave them up to uncleanness, first of all (v. 24). Paul has in mind all kinds of uncleanness but especially sexual uncleanness. Second, he gave them up to vile affections (v. 26). This means sexual perversions. Third, he gave them up to a reprobate mind (v. 28).

Would you not think that a reprobate mind should come first? Years ago I would have thought perhaps that the order was not quite right, or at least I would not have understood it. But I do not think that way anymore. The reason I do not think that way anymore is that I now recognize that this is the way depravity progresses. First there is uncleanness. For example, fornication and adultery. After this come sexual perversions: prostitution and homosexuality. Then what? What follows is a reprobate mind, whereby men and women, who should be ashamed of the things they are doing, say instead, "Not only are we doing these things and will continue to do them, but we consider that these things are right and demand that you recognize that they are right." That is the progression in Romans 1.

It is exactly what we have happening in our own time—not just in our culture but also in our churches. What is the significance of the movement in our day in which the gay community is demanding ordination to the Christian ministry? Is it a question of minority rights? Not at all! Not in the slightest! Rather, it is the gay community coming to the churches as the only recognized moral authority in the land (though they are scarcely that) to say, "We want you to declare before your people and the world that what we do is right." It is the expression of the reprobate mind.

If Romans 1 is the Word of God and if it is trustworthy (which it is), then what we are witnessing in our day in the churches is God giving them up to this kind of thing. It is bad enough to be given up to sexual uncleanness. It is worse to be given up to sexual perversion. But it is worst of all to be given up to that kind of mind that says, "I demand that you, God, recognize that what I in my depravity want to do is right."

Understand that I am not just talking about homosexuality as if this is the most terrible sin there is. There are all kinds of sins, and who is to say which sin is most terrible? It is just that this is the clearest illustration of the principle in our time. If you are an adulterer and are asking God to justify your adultery, you are just as bad. If you are a thief and are asking God to justify your stealing, you are just as bad. That is the lowest point to which God can give us up. When he does, we become by virtue of that judgment even worse than the thing to which we are compared.

Lower Than the Beasts

In Psalm 8:4–5 (Heb. 2:6–7) there is a description of man that reads, "What is man that you are mindful of him, the son of man that you care for him? You made him a little lower than the heavenly beings and crowned him with glory and honor." These verses fix man in an interesting place in God's created order: lower than the angels, but higher than the beasts—somewhere between. It is the glory of men and women in that position that, as God speaks to them and reveals himself to them, they can look up to God and the angels, rather than down. But you see, if you will not look up, you will inevitably look down, and you will become like the one to whom you are looking. If you look to God, you will become like God. If you will not look to God and worship God, you will not become like God; you will become like beasts.

There has been something very interesting in the papers recently. We have an evolutionary naturalistic philosophy in our day, and part of this philosophy, we are to understand, is that men and women are only well-developed animals. Therefore, when we want to justify what used to be called "perversions," the way to do it is to show that animals do it too. Because, after all, it is "just our background." I have noticed a number of articles that are trying to find in the animal world justification for our perverted behavior.

Not long ago an article appeared on a certain kind of duck. It has within its duck community something approaching gang rape, at least according to the thesis of the people who observed it and wrote the article. I think the idea was, "Look, it's not so bad to have gang rape because even the ducks do it." Well, it may be—I do not know; I have not observed this particular family of ducks—it may be that something like this happens in the duck world. But you have to go far and wide before you can find anything like that in the animal world, and you find it everywhere in the human race.

A story of a similar nature appeared in the September 6, 1982, issue of *Newsweek* magazine. It was accompanied by a picture of a baboon presumably killing an infant baboon, and over this was a headline that read: "Biologists Say Infanticide Is as Normal as the Sex Drive—And That Most Animals, Including Man, Practice It." The implication of the title is obvious. Man is an animal. Other animals kill their young. Therefore, it is all right for humans to kill their young also. But, of course, the whole thing is fallacious. Most animals do not kill their offspring. And even if they do, it is nothing to compare to the systematic murder by abortion of one and a half million babies each year in the United States alone—in most instances, simply for the convenience of the mother.

Besides, human beings are not animals. Humans are made in the image of God and have the opportunity of looking up to him and becoming increasingly like him through his grace in Jesus Christ. But if we will not look up, if we will not become like God, we will inevitably look down and increasingly become like the animals.

Indeed, we will become worse than the animals, which is what Nebuchadnezzar's fall indicates. If you say, "Look how good I am; look at what I have done," if you do not give God the glory, you will bring ruin upon yourself because God rules in the affairs of men and has ordained that this should be so.

How Low Can You Go?

I have spoken individually. But let me say that this happens nationally as well. I am interested to follow the moral tone of our nation, and in my opinion, it is going down so quickly it is hard to keep up. As I read the papers week after week, I ask at what point, if any, in the moral decline of our time, people will pull back and say, "This is just terrible! We will not go this far." The point is certainly not adultery; we have plenty of that. It is not even prostitution; we have movements to recognize prostitution, even legalize it, if possible. The point is not even pornography. But I have noticed in recent years that there has been an attempt to say, "Well, the point at which we will draw the line is *child* pornography. Adults can do what they want; we must not be intolerant. Grown-ups can go to hell if they want to go to hell. But not children."

Well, that sounds good. At least there is a point beyond which we will not go. But is that the case? Look at the movie *Pretty Baby*. It starred Brooke Shields, who at the time she made it was twelve years old. It was a classy movie, not a dirty pornographic movie. But it was about a twelve-year-old girl who is a child prostitute in a brothel in New Orleans and who perhaps "matures" through the experience.

Do you see what I am saying? If we will not have God, there is no point at which we can stop in the moral decline. God is the only one who can hold his creatures up and remold them by grace into the image of Jesus Christ. Therefore, if we will not have him and instead turn to our own way, we will go down, down, down individually and nationally as well. That is happening. It is happening here and elsewhere in the world.

Light Bearers

Let me suggest our proper role by this contrast. When I was talking about Satan and his rebellion, I pointed out that his sin was taking God's glory to himself. If we want to see the role that we *should* have, we need only go back before the fall of Satan to what he was doing for God before he sinned. In Ezekiel 28 the prophet describes Satan as standing upon the holy mount of

God directing the worship of the creation to God and interpreting the demands of God to the creation. His name was Lucifer then. It meant "light bearer." He was the one who bore the worship of the creation up to God and then reflected God's image back to the creation.

That is our role as Christian people—not to take the glory to ourselves but rather to achieve everything we possibly can achieve, to do as well as we possibly can do, to be as moral as we possibly can be, and then when we are as moral and as successful as we possibly can be, to point to God and say, "It is not I, but Christ who works in me."

Nebuchadnezzar, I think, finally got the message, because at the very end of Daniel 4 he confesses that the God whom earlier he had called Daniel's God is now his God as well. Notice verse 34: "My sanity was restored. Then I praised the Most High; I honored and glorified him who lives forever." Then verse 37, which contains the very last words we hear from Nebuchadnezzar: "Now I, Nebuchadnezzar, praise and exalt and glorify the King of heaven, because everything he does is right and all his ways are just. And those who walk in pride he is able to humble."

God is not only able to humble them; he does humble them. But as we humble ourselves, we find ourselves exalted in the role God has called us to fill, that of light bearers, reflectors of the glory of God. We find that God uses people as inconspicuous and unimpressive as ourselves to bring people, even like Nebuchadnezzar, to the knowledge of himself.

7

Belshazzar Gave a Party

Daniel 5:1–31

O king, the Most High God gave your father Nebuchadnezzar sovereignty and greatness and glory and splendor. Because of the high position he gave him, all the peoples and nations and men of every language dreaded and feared him. Those the king wanted to put to death, he put to death; those he wanted to spare, he spared; those he wanted to promote, he promoted; and those he wanted to humble, he humbled. But when his heart became arrogant and hardened with pride, he was deposed from his royal throne and stripped of his glory. He was driven away from people and given the mind of an animal; he lived with the wild donkeys and ate grass like cattle; and his body was drenched with the dew of heaven, until he acknowledged that the Most High God is sovereign over the kingdoms of men and sets over them anyone he wishes.

But you his son, O Belshazzar, have not humbled yourself, though you knew all this. Instead, you have set yourself up against the Lord of heaven. You had the goblets from his temple brought to you, and you and your nobles, your wives and your concubines drank wine from them. You praised the gods of silver and gold, of bronze, iron, wood and stone, which cannot see or hear or understand. But you did not honor the God who holds in his hand your life and all your ways. Therefore he sent the hand that wrote the inscription.

This is the inscription that was written:

MENE, MENE, TEKEL, PARSIN

This is what these words mean:

> *Mene: God has numbered the days of your reign and brought it to an end.*
>
> *Tekel: You have been weighed on the scales and found wanting.*
>
> *Peres: Your kingdom is divided and given to the Medes and Persians. . . .*

That very night Belshazzar, king of the Babylonians, was slain, and Darius the Mede took over the kingdom, at the age of sixty-two.

Belshazzar gave a party, and he invited all his friends." I do not often remember exact sentences of sermons I have heard preached, but I do remember that one. It was the way Billy Graham began a sermon on Daniel years ago. "Belshazzar gave a party!" What a party it was! The king assembled one thousand of his nobles, plus many wives and concubines. Wine flowed. The palace roared with laughter. At the height of the party, Belshazzar called for the gold and silver goblets that his predecessor King Nebuchadnezzar had taken from the great temple at Jerusalem years before, and he and his nobles, his wives and his concubines drank from the goblets and praised the gods of Babylon—gods of gold and silver, of bronze, iron, wood, and stone.

Suddenly a disembodied hand appeared and began to write on the wall. The king and his nobles believed in dark omens, and this was the most unusual and terrifying omen they had ever seen. We are told that the king's "face turned pale and he was so frightened that his knees knocked together and his legs gave way" (Dan. 5:6).

Belshazzar called for the enchanters and diviners to read the writing and explain what it meant, but they were baffled. At last Daniel, who by the time of this story had become a much older man, was summoned, and he read the writing. It was a judgment.

> O king, the Most High God gave your father Nebuchadnezzar sovereignty and greatness and glory and splendor. . . . But when his heart became arrogant and hardened with pride, he was deposed from his royal throne and stripped of his glory. He was driven away from people and given the mind of an animal; he lived with the wild donkeys and ate grass like cattle; and his body was drenched with the dew of heaven, until he acknowledged that the Most High God is sovereign over the kingdoms of men and sets over them anyone he wishes. But you his son, O Belshazzar, have not humbled yourself, though you knew all this.
>
> verses 18, 20–21

Then Daniel read the inscription: MENE, MENE, TEKEL, PARSIN.

He explained it. *Mene* meant "God has numbered the days of your reign and brought it to an end" (v. 26). *Tekel* meant "You have been weighed on the scales and found wanting" (v. 27). *Peres* meant "Your kingdom is divided and given to the Medes and Persians" (v. 28).

And so it happened! That night Darius the Mede attacked Babylon and overthrew it, killing Belshazzar. It was an example of God's great judgments in human history and is a warning to all.

Who Was Belshazzar?

Before I deal with the meaning of this judgment, I want to discuss Belshazzar himself. This is because the name Belshazzar—or the lack of the name Belshazzar in historical records—became a basis for many strong liberal attacks on the authenticity of Daniel in past years.

The chief extrabiblical supply of information about ancient Babylon is the Greek historian Brosius, who is quoted by Flavius Josephus as the source of his information. The problem is that Brosius does not mention Belshazzar as one of Babylon's kings. In fact, he does not mention the name Belshazzar at all, nor (for many years) was the name found anywhere. Nebuchadnezzar was known. So were the names of three kings who succeeded him in rather rapid succession. But the last of these was Nabonidus, and Belshazzar is not mentioned. Liberal scholars picked up on the theory of the third-century Phoenician philosopher Porphyry that Daniel was actually written about 165 B.C., long after the events it supposedly describes, and that it has little, if any, historical information. In 1850 one commentator, Ferdinand Hitzig, declared that Belshazzar was clearly a figment of the writer's imagination.[1]

But, as usual, time has a way of overturning such theories. In this case, in 1854 a British consul named J. G. Taylor was exploring some ruins in southern Iraq for the British Museum and came across several small cylinders inscribed with sixty or so lines of cuneiform writing. It turned out that the inscriptions had been written at the command of Nabonidus, who ruled Babylon from 555 to 539 B.C. They commemorated the repair of a temple tower at Ur, and they contained a prayer for the long life and good health of Nabonidus *and for his eldest son Belshazzar.* So for the first time the name Belshazzar was discovered in an ancient extrabiblical record, and it was proved that he was an important person who lived in Babylon at the time of its fall.

Still, Belshazzar was only identified as the eldest son of Nabonidus and not as a king of Babylon. In fact, since Taylor's discovery in 1854, several other Babylonian remains have been found that also mention Belshazzar. But he is always called the king's son or the crown prince, not king. How then are we to explain the identification of Belshazzar as "king" in Daniel 5:1?

I quote here from the May-June 1985 issue of *Biblical Archeology Review.*

In legal deeds from the sixth century B.C. the parties swear oaths by the gods and the king, according to a well-known and long-standing practice. In some of these deeds from the reign of Nabonidus, we find that the parties swear by Nabonidus and by Belshazzar, the king's son. This formula, swearing by the king and his son, is unattested in any other reign in any documents yet uncovered. This suggests that Belshazzar may have had a special status. We know that during part of his father's reign, Belshazzar was the effective authority in Babylon. The Babylonian texts reveal that Nabonidus was an eccentric ruler. While he did not ignore the gods of Babylon, he did not treat them in the

approved way, and gave very considerable attention to the moon god at two
other cities, Ur and Harran. For several years of his reign, Nabonidus did not
even live in Babylon; instead he stayed at the distant oasis of Teima in northern Arabia. During that time, Belshazzar ruled in Babylon. According to one
account, Nabonidus "entrusted the kingship" to Belshazzar.[2]

Apparently, as Herodotus, the Greek historian, suggests, Nabonidus with
his armies left Babylon to fight against Darius. He was defeated by Darius
and fled to Borsippa, where he was bottled up by some of Darius's troops.
Then Darius advanced against Babylon where Belshazzar was apparently
reigning in his father's absence. The events of Daniel 5 took place on the
night of the city's fall.

Besides, there is this point: In Daniel 5:16, Belshazzar offers to make Daniel
"the third highest ruler in the kingdom" if he can read and interpret the
writing on the wall. Why "third" highest? When Pharaoh offered a similar
reward to Joseph, it was to make him second only to Pharaoh (Gen. 41:40,
44). Why should Belshazzar have offered to make Daniel third in command
in an exactly parallel situation? The puzzle is explained if we conclude, as
apparently we should, that Belshazzar was himself actually only the second
ruler in the kingdom, even though he was at that time the acting king of
Babylon. Since Belshazzar's father, Nabonidus, was still living, Belshazzar
would have been able only to offer the third place to Daniel.

I have said many times that if you want to look very wise in the world's
eyes and are willing to risk looking foolish years from now, you can make a
reputation for yourself by pointing out the "errors" in the Bible. There are
always facts we do not know and things we fail to understand, so it will always
be possible to point to certain items and say that they are errors. But these
things tend to become explained. As time passes and the data from archaeology, historical investigations, numismatics, and other disciplines accumu-
late, these alleged "errors" tend to explode in the faces of those who pro-
pound them, and the position of these who have taken their stand upon the
historical accuracy and inerrancy of this book is vindicated. The Bible is seen
to be more reliable, not less reliable, as time passes.

Sin and Judgment

There are a number of important lessons in this story, however—quite
beyond the lesson of the Bible's reliability. Let me give them briefly and then
apply them in a slightly wider way.

First, *sin is not static.* That is, the one who sins never remains on a plateau.
The path of sin always leads downhill, as we saw also in the last chapter. In
the case of Belshazzar, because he would not learn from the example and
experience of his predecessor Nebuchadnezzar, Belshazzar sank not merely
to Nebuchadnezzar's insane bestiality, which was a punishment for his arrogance, but lower still. Nebuchadnezzar sinned by boasting, "Is not this the

great Babylon I have built as the royal residence, by my mighty power and for the glory of my majesty?" (Dan. 4:30). He took to himself the glory due God and was punished by God by the loss of his reason. Belshazzar went further. He blasphemed God by desecrating the vessels of God taken from the temple at Jerusalem and by praising idols in the true God's place. He was punished not merely by the loss of his reason (though his actions were a true insanity) but also by the loss of his kingdom and his life.

This is the biblical pattern. It was the pattern of Gomer, who left Hosea to live with other men.

It was the pattern of Jonah, whose rejection of God's call led to near disaster.

The pattern is enunciated clearly in Romans 1:

Although they knew God, they neither glorified him as God nor gave thanks to him, but their thinking became futile and their foolish hearts were darkened. Although they claimed to be wise, they became fools and exchanged the glory of the immortal God for images made to look like mortal man and birds and animals and reptiles. Therefore God gave them over in the sinful desires of their hearts to sexual impurity . . . to shameful lusts . . . [and] to a depraved mind.

verses 21–24, 26, 28

This is exactly what Daniel told Belshazzar. "But you his son, O Belshazzar, have not humbled yourself, though you knew all this" (Dan. 5:22).

Second, *sin makes us impervious to danger.* Karl Marx said that "religion is the opiate of the people." He meant that religion puts us to sleep so that our oppressors have less trouble maintaining their supremacy. But Marx got it exactly backward. It is not religion that drugs us; it is sin. True religion wakes us up by turning us from sin to the righteousness of God that is in Jesus Christ.

Belshazzar's final fling is an example of this stupidity. Darius was outside the walls. That very night he would dam up the river and enter the city through the space provided when the water dropped and exposed the portals through which the river entered Babylon. At the moment of this greatest of all dangers, Belshazzar was drugging himself at his party. Yet it is not only Belshazzar who has done this. Our culture is doing it as well. Some time ago a book by Neil Postman, entitled *Amusing Ourselves to Death: Public Discourse in the Age of Show Business,* appeared in American bookstores. It was about television and its pernicious effects on our country. It might well have been written about culture at large and have voiced alarm at our spiritual condition. By refusing to think, especially about eternal realities, and by filling our days with entertainment, particularly sin-oriented entertainment, we lose sight of danger and plunge into the abyss.

Third, *God is not static.* I have said that sin is not static, but I need to say also that God is not static. There are times in history when sin abounds and God does not seem to intervene—at least not spectacularly. But we must not think that God is unaffected by sin or that he will ignore it forever simply because his judgments are postponed. In times like these the wrath of God accumulates, like waters rising behind a dam. The time eventually comes when that great accumulation of wrath is poured out against sinners. This happens to nations at the moments of their greatest arrogance. It happens to individuals. It happens when the judgments of God are least expected.

I think of how Jesus spoke in his Olivet discourse just before his crucifixion.

> As it was in the days of Noah, so it will be at the coming of the Son of Man. For in the days before the flood, people were eating and drinking, marrying and giving in marriage, up to the day Noah entered the ark; and they knew nothing about what would happen until the flood came and took them all away. That is how it will be at the coming of the Son of Man. Two men will be in the field; one will be taken and the other left. Two women will be grinding with a hand mill; one will be taken and the other left. Therefore keep watch, because you do not know on what day your Lord will come. . . . Be ready, because the Son of Man will come at an hour when you do not expect him.
>
> Matthew 24:37–42, 44

The only thing more certain for us than death and taxes is the final judgment.

The Final Judgment

This leads to a consideration of the final judgment itself. I begin by pointing out that this conclusion to a study of the fall of Babylon to Darius is not something I am importing into the story but rather is itself a biblical comparison. If you know the content of the Book of Revelation, you know that in the seventeenth through the nineteenth chapters the final judgment of God on evil is represented pictorially as the fall of "mystery Babylon" (Rev. 17:5). The lament begins: "Fallen! Fallen is Babylon the Great!" (Rev. 18:2). At her fall the kings of earth, who have shared in her sins, cry out: "Woe! Woe, O great city" (v. 10). The merchants, who have profited from her commerce, and the sea captains, who have grown rich on her conquests, also cry: "Woe! Woe, O great city" (vv. 16, 19). It is a scene of utter dismay and anguish.

But in the next chapter we find not mourning but rejoicing, as the saints of God express their emotions at this judgment.

> Hallelujah!
> Salvation and glory and power belong to our God,
>   for true and just are his judgments.
> He has condemned the great prostitute
>   who corrupted the earth by her adulteries.
> He has avenged on her the blood of his servants.
>
> Revelation 19:1–2

Again they shout:

> Hallelujah!
> The smoke from her goes up for ever and ever.
>
> verse 3

And again,

> Amen, Hallelujah!
>
> verse 4

Here the Bible links the final judgment to the fall of ancient Babylon, using the earlier fall as a portrait of all sinners' destinies. *And this is good!* We tend to sentimentalize evil. But God tells us that evil will be judged and that the saints will rejoice in this judgment, even as good people rejoiced in the fall of Belshazzar and his wicked regime.

But I must also say that God does not get a kick out of the damnation of the wicked. He tells us these things so that we might turn from sin to salvation as provided in Jesus Christ.

Let me present the case in this way. The day is coming—it may not be far off—when you and I and all persons are going to stand before the judgment seat of God. God is our king. But you are a rebellious subject. God is righteous, but you are a sinner. You are to be weighed in that judgment, and the judgment of God written over you is going to be the judgment of God on Belshazzar's Babylon: MENE, MENE, TEKEL, PARSIN.

Mene means that God is going to number your deeds to show that you have failed to achieve his standards. We are told in Revelation of a great book in which the deeds of men and women are recorded. This book will be opened on the day of judgment, and the evil you have done will be poured out on one side of God's scales. That is what the word *tekel* signifies. All the lies, all the hypocrisies, all the self-seeking, all the harm done to others—all this will fill the scale. You will be weighed. And as you stand there that great scale of God is going to go crashing down on the side of your just doom and condemnation.

Then God is going to speak the word *peres:* divided. The Greek word for judgment means "divided," for God's judgment is a final dividing of the ways. One way leads to life; the other leads to the outer darkness of hell "where there will be weeping and gnashing of teeth" and "eternal punishment" (Matt. 25:30, 46).

What will you say in that day? How will you respond when God measures your deeds, weighs your character, and declares you wanting?

Left to yourself there will be nothing for you to do and nothing to say in response. But God has done something at the point of your inability. God has sent the Lord Jesus Christ to die in your place, taking the full punishment of your sin upon himself. Jesus has made it possible for God to apply his righteousness to your account. You have no righteousness of your own—not as God counts righteousness. But God takes those scales, brushes your evil deeds aside as having been punished on your behalf in Jesus Christ, and on the other side of the scale he places his own character. The scales swing back, and you are justified on the basis of Christ's righteousness.

You must trust him. You must turn from unrighteousness. Will you? There is no better time to do it than right now.

8

A Busy Man's Devotional Life

Daniel 6:1–28

It pleased Darius to appoint 120 satraps to rule throughout the kingdom, with three administrators over them, one of whom was Daniel. The satraps were made accountable to them so that the king might not suffer loss. Now Daniel so distinguished himself among the administrators and the satraps by his exceptional qualities that the king planned to set him over the whole kingdom. At this, the administrators and the satraps tried to find grounds for charges against Daniel in his conduct of government affairs, but they were unable to do so. They could find no corruption in him, because he was trustworthy and neither corrupt nor negligent. Finally these men said, "We will never find any basis for charges against this man Daniel unless it has something to do with the law of his God."

There is a verse in the sixth chapter of Daniel that I wish could be spoken of every believer in the Lord Jesus Christ, though I confess that it probably cannot be. Daniel had been promoted to a position of great prominence, and those around him were jealous. They wanted to find something for which to accuse him and pull him down. They could not. Finally they confessed, "We will never find any basis for charges against this man Daniel unless it has something to do with the law of his God" (v. 5).

Is that not wonderful? Would it not be wonderful if that could be said of every Christian, especially of us? I am afraid that it cannot usually be said of us, because there are many things of which we can rightly be accused.

At times we can be accused of wrong actions. The world says, "That Christian is doing something that is not right. His (or her) actions are against

65

what all people everywhere believe in." If this is the case with us, we need to
confess the sin and have it cleansed and forgiven by Jesus Christ. At other
times we can be accused of laziness. The jealous peers of Daniel tried to fault
him for negligence (v. 4), but they could not prove that he had been ne-
glectful of anything. Sometimes people accuse Christians of pride. They say,
"Those Christians are no better than we are. In fact, they are much worse.
They sin and are lazy, and then, to top it all off, they are proud of being like
that." This may be an unjust accusation in some instances, but Christians
sometimes have been prideful.

Are we? If so, perhaps it will yet be said of us—even if it cannot properly
be said of us at this moment—perhaps as the result of this study, "We will
never find any basis for a charge against these people unless it has something to do with the law of their God."

Who Was Darius?

The story in which this comment is made is the best-known story in Daniel
and one of the best-known stories in the Old Testament. It involves Daniel's
being thrown into a den of lions, and according to Daniel 5:31, it takes place
under the reign of Darius, who succeeded Belshazzar as the ruler of Babylon.

But there is a problem here. You will remember from our study of chapter 5 that Darius's predecessor as king of Babylon, Belshazzar, was not known
from archaeological or historical records until the middle of the last century. As a result, many scholars argued that Belshazzar never existed. They
assert that the author of Daniel actually wrote much later than the book purports to have been written, that he merely invented Belshazzar for his own
theological or polemical reasons. This theory has been discredited, as we
saw. Belshazzar did exist, and he did reign in Babylon. But I review this problem to say that a similar situation exists in the case of Darius. Only in Darius's
case to date no reference to "Darius the Mede" has been discovered as the
result of archaeology. In fact, reference to Darius's conquering Babylon even
seems to be wrong, because the historical records give that honor to a general of Cyrus named Ugbaru.

What is the solution? So far three possible solutions have been offered.

1. *Daniel is mistaken.* This is the liberal solution, and it is consistent with
liberal proclivities to late dating and the denial of the possibility of predictive prophecy. The liberal theory is that Daniel was written at the time of the
Maccabees, about 165 B.C. According to this idea, the author mistakenly supposed that it was a ruler of the Medes who conquered Babylon (rather than
Cyrus the Persian). He then also wrongly attributed the conquest to a later
Darius, Darius the Great (522–484 B.C.), who followed Cyrus's son Cambyses
as king of Babylon. However, liberal scholars have a hidden agenda in this
proposal. If they can assign the writing of the book to the time of the
Maccabees and separate the Medes from the Persians as world rulers, then
they can account for the four kingdoms of Nebuchadnezzar's dream as (1)

the Chaldeans, (2) the Medes, (3) the Persians, and (4) the Greeks; thus, all the kingdoms would have come on the stage of history by the time of the book's writing. There is no need for predictive prophecy. If this set of identifications does not work, then the fourth kingdom must be the kingdom of Rome, and that would still be a future, prophesied kingdom even by the liberal scholars' own late dating.

But the liberal explanation is wrong. No writer of the time could have made such a serous mistake and still have retained credibility. Gleason L. Archer puts the case like this:

> Such confusion as to the true nationality and time sequence of Darius the Great would have been unthinkable in the second-century B.C. Hellenistic world; for even in the Near East every schoolboy was required to read Xenophon, if not Herodotus, and other Greek historians from the fifth and fourth centuries B.C. Even in Hellenistic Palestine, these authors were widely read and admired. It is from Xenophon and Herodotus that we gain our information concerning Cyrus and Darius. Any Greek-writing author, or author within the Hellenistic orbit, who attempted to put Darius before Cyrus would have been laughed off the stage by the general public; and no credence would have been given to anything he wrote.[1]

We can conclude that Darius the Mede and Darius the Great have nothing to do with each other and that the liberal scholars are wrong both in their theory that the author of Daniel confused the two and in their late dating.

2. *Darius is Ugbaru.* Ugbaru was the general of Cyrus who engineered the fall of Babylon, and it is believed that he was appointed king of Babylon by Cyrus, who was urgently needed on another front shortly after taking over the capital. Ugbaru reigned in Babylon for about a year until Cyrus returned and was himself crowned king, later transferring the title to Cambyses. This is the explanation offered by Robert Dick Wilson, the great Old Testament scholar at Princeton Theological Seminary a generation or so ago; C. F. Keil, coauthor with F. Delitzsch of the famous *Biblical Commentaries on the Old Testament;* William Foxwell Albright, who started out as a liberal scholar but became increasingly conservative as the result of his archaeological investigations; and Gleason L. Archer, whose work I have just quoted.

There is good support for this position. Daniel 9:1 says that Darius "was made ruler" over Babylon. This verse uses the passive stem of the verb *homlak* rather than the more normal active form of the verb *malak*, which would have been used if Darius had obtained the throne by his own conquest or by inheritance. Again, although the New International Version does not reflect this, the Aramaic text of Daniel 5:31 actually says that Darius "received" the kingship, as if it had been granted him by a higher authority. These terms are used for the appointment of vassal kings. A third argument in support of this explanation is that Daniel never mentions more than the "first year" of Darius's reign, perhaps indicating that it was of short duration.

Why then does Daniel call Ugbaru, Darius? We do not know the answer to that question. But ancient kings often had more than one name—just as Daniel himself had more than one name, being Daniel to the Jews and Belteshadnezzar to King Nebuchadnezzar. Besides, it is possible that Darius is derived from the Persian word *dara*, which means "king," in which case the name may have been only an honorary title.

3. *Darius is Cyrus*. The third explanation is similar to the second, only in this case Darius is identified with Cyrus himself. This view was advanced by D. T. Wiseman. It might be argued that Daniel 6:28 refutes this theory, for that verse says, "So Daniel prospered during the reign of Darius and the reign of Cyrus the Persian." It seems to distinguish between the two kings. But this may be a case in which the connecting word "and" should be taken in the sense of "even" or "that is." The verse could read: "So Daniel prospered during the reign of Darius, even [or 'that is'] the reign of Cyrus the Persian." If this is right, the verse would actually explain who Darius was.

I do not know which of these second two explanations should be preferred, though the identification of Darius with Ugbaru seems best in my judgment. But I do know that it is wise to show humility in such matters and wait expectantly until further data come in. As in the case of Belshazzar, a discovery may yet explain who Darius was. Until then it is wise to trust the biblical narrative. There is no real reason for doubting the historical reliability of this or any other biblical book.

The Assault on Daniel

So we return to the story of Daniel and his jealous accusers, and we note that if his enemies were going to be able to attack him at all, it was going to have to be in the area of his relationship to God. Daniel must have been over eighty years old at this time; these men had had many years to observe him. Yet there was nothing they could honestly accuse him of. So they resorted to a stratagem. They approached Darius with the flattering suggestion that a law be passed according to which no one would be allowed to pray to any god or man for the next thirty days, except to Darius himself. They suggested further that if anyone should disobey the law, he should be thrown into a den of hungry lions. It was proposed that this be done in a most binding way, according to the laws of the Medes and Persians, which could not be annulled.

Darius was trapped by this evil plot. He did not want to condemn Daniel, but he easily fell into this deception.

What did it mean for Darius to issue a law forbidding anyone to pray to any god or man except himself for a period of thirty days? The answer is obvious. It meant that Darius was putting himself in the place of God—unwittingly perhaps, but nevertheless doing so. He was saying, "I am the one to whom people should look for all things. I am sovereign." This is what Belshazzar had done in the desecration of the temple vessels and what

Nebuchadnezzar had done before him. It was the ultimate blasphemy, the sin God will not tolerate.

But this is the sin of every secular culture—the sin of putting self in God's place. We have expressions of this in Babylon. But think also of the kingdom of Rome whose coming Daniel prophesied. Rome was extraordinarily arrogant, and the ultimate arrogance was the cult of the Caesars. Citizens of the empire were required to burn a pinch of incense to the reigning Caesar and utter the words *Kyrios Kaisar* ("Caesar is Lord!"). It is this that the early Christians refused to do and for which they were themselves thrown to the wild lions or crucified. It was not that Christians were forbidden to worship God. They were free to worship any god they chose so long as they also acknowledged Caesar. Romans were tolerant. But when Christians denied to Caesar the allegiance that they believed belonged to the true God only, they were executed.

Is it any different today? We think that we are in a more enlightened age, and we are in some respects. In most places in the world a person is not killed for an exclusive worship of Jesus Christ. But there are different kinds of executions, and the attacks on Christians are often no less vicious than the attack on Daniel.

Here is an example. In early 1981, after Ronald Reagan's election as president of the United States, the distinguished pediatric surgeon C. Everett Koop was appointed Deputy Assistant Secretary of Health and Human Services, which put him in line to become Surgeon General of the United States. Koop was then Surgeon-in-Chief of Children's Hospital in Philadelphia, where the entire surgical center is named in his honor. He is a pioneer in pediatric surgery and an inventor of many pediatric surgical techniques. He founded and was at that time editor of the *Journal of Pediatric Surgery*. He had been awarded the French *Legion d'Honneur*.

But Koop opposed abortion on the grounds that the fetus is made in the image of God and that to abort it is to commit murder. Indeed, he was nominated to be Surgeon General because of this conviction. But because his opposition to abortion was unpopular at that time, the media especially, but also many political opponents, embarked on a scurrilous campaign in which his many medical accomplishments were ignored and he was repeatedly portrayed as little more than a close-minded fundamentalist. The *Washington Post* described him as "a fundamentalist Christian with a Lincolnesque beard . . . the narrator of a controversial anti-abortion film, *Whatever Happened to the Human Race?*" (March 6, 1981). The *Boston Globe* dismissed him as a mere "clinician . . . with tunnel vision."[2]

These and other attacks delayed Koop's appointment as Surgeon General for nearly a year, although in the end he was appointed. Today, of course, attitudes on abortion have changed substantially in some quarters. But in 1981 this was a clear case of our own society wanting to continue to play God in the matter of the life of the unborn, and of its furious hostility against anyone, however distinguished, who stood against it in obedience to God.

If we practice our religion on the reservation and do not attempt to bring it out into the real world, the world will tolerate us. But if we determine to take a stand on any important issue on the basis of genuine religious principle, the fury of our secular society will break all bounds.

The Practice of God's Presence

Daniel was an experienced courtier, so he knew at once what the king's decree meant—and where it came from. For thirty days Daniel would need to abandon his customary practice of praying thrice daily before his open window in the direction of Jerusalem, or else be thrown into the den of lions. *For thirty days!* "Well," we say, "that's not too bad." It isn't as if he had to bow down to an idol as his friends Shadrach, Meshach, and Abednego were required to do. All he had to do was stop praying openly for one month. Indeed, he could be subtle. He could close his window so his prayers would not be seen or, better yet, pray in bed at night. He could let his devotions slide for a month. After all, there are many so-called Christians today who probably allow a month or more to slide by without any significant devotions.

We may think like that. Doubtless many do. But not Daniel! Instead we read that "when Daniel learned that the decree had been published, he went home to his upstairs room where the windows opened toward Jerusalem. Three times a day he got down on his knees and prayed, giving thanks to his God, just as he had done before" (Dan. 6:10).

I like those last words: "just as he had done before." This was a pattern with Daniel. The outside world may have been changing, but God had not changed and Daniel was not going to allow his relationship to God to change regardless of the shifting circumstances.

I want you to see two things about Daniel at this point. First, Daniel was the smallest of all possible minorities at this time—a minority of one—but although he was only one man among many hostile enemies, *he was the one man who knew the true state of affairs in this struggle.* Darius did not know what was going on. He had not even been able to see through the strategy of the administrators and satraps, and he perceived nothing of the spiritual struggle. The conspirators did not understand the situation. They did not know Daniel's God, and they thought it would be an easy thing to get Daniel executed.

At this time Daniel probably did not even have the support of his three friends, for they are not mentioned as they were in the incident involving Nebuchadnezzar's dream (cf. Dan. 2:17–18). Either they had been transferred to other parts of the empire or they had died; Daniel was now elderly. Here was one man standing alone in the midst of an utterly pagan culture. All were against him. Any who knew his convictions would have laughed at them. Yet in all this vast empire Daniel was the one man who really had it together. He knew that there was a true God, and he knew who that true God was. He knew that God was powerful. He knew that God could deliver him, if he chose to do so. Above all, he knew that obeying and serving the one true God had to be the supreme goal in his life.

That leads to the second important thing about Daniel, namely, *what he knew he practiced openly.* Some people maintain their belief in God privately and confess him if asked. But they do not want to offend anyone. They do not want to be seen as religious. So they back off. They retreat. They privatize their convictions. Daniel did not do that, and in this he showed true greatness. Instead of hiding his convictions, he knelt before his window in the sight of Babylon and prayed as he had always done.

We need more Daniels. We need more people who are willing to bring their awareness of God and his laws off the reservation, who are willing to open their windows and honor him before a watching world.

Safe in Babylon

The end of this story is the least interesting part, because we know it already. Darius did not want to see Daniel killed. So he tried to find means to escape the force of the unchangeable edict, to no avail. The law had to be enforced. So at last the king had Daniel thrown to the lions, calling out, "May your God, whom you serve continually, rescue you!" (Dan. 6:16).

There is a point from an earlier moment in the story that is of interest now. When the conspirators burst in upon Daniel while he was praying, we are told that they found him "asking God for help" (v. 11). This means that Daniel was not oblivious to his danger, even though his outward calm might have suggested that he was not taking the threat of execution seriously. Actually, Daniel was acutely aware of his danger. He knew that he stood to lose his life. He was asking God to help him. But, of course, that is exactly what God did. God stopped the lions' mouths so they could not attack Daniel, and while Daniel was with them he was kept from harm not only from the lions but from his enemies too. They could not get to him. He was in the safest place in all Babylon, and that night (I am sure) Daniel slept marvelously.

It was the king who could not sleep. He thrashed about, and very early in the morning he rushed to the lions' den to see what had become of his most influential administrator. "Daniel, servant of the living God, has your God, whom you serve continually, been able to rescue you from the lions?" (v. 20).

What kind of answer do you think Darius was expecting? "Grrr" from the lions? I do not know. But I do know that the lions were silent. God had shut their mouths. So when Daniel spoke he was heard clearly. "O king, live forever! My God sent his angel, and he shut the mouths of the lions. They have not hurt me, because I was found innocent in his sight. Nor have I ever done any wrong before you, O king" (vv. 21–22). The king had Daniel drawn from the den. He had the conspirators and their families thrown into it. Then he issued a decree with which the story ends:

> For he is the living God
> and he endures forever;
> his kingdom will not be destroyed,
> his dominion will never end.
> He rescues and he saves;
> he performs signs and wonders
> in the heavens and on the earth.
> He has rescued Daniel
> from the power of the lions.
>
> verses 26–27

It was not a very profound decree, but it was profound for the king and it was certainly true enough. It is true today. God is God and he had rescued Daniel.

We must say in all honesty that God does not always rescue his servants in this fashion. Hebrews 11:33 speaks of those who by faith "shut the mouths of lions," a clear reference to Daniel. But immediately after that the book also speaks of those who "were tortured and refused to be released . . . faced jeers and flogging . . . were stoned . . . were sawed in two . . . were put to death by the sword" and suffered other punishments (vv. 35–37).

God calls some to win by living. Others are called to win by dying. But in life or death God rules and we are called to serve him. Will we do it? The world needs those who know God and who will live for his righteousness even when the entire culture turns ferociously against it.

9

History by the Ounce

Daniel 7:1-28

In the first year of Belshazzar king of Babylon, Daniel had a dream, and visions passed through his mind as he was lying on his bed. He wrote down the substance of his dream.

Daniel said: "In my vision at night I looked, and there before me were the four winds of heaven churning up the great sea. Four great beasts, each different from the others, came up out of the sea.

"The first was like a lion, and it had the wings of an eagle. I watched until its wings were torn off and it was lifted from the ground so that it stood on two feet like a man, and the heart of a man was given to it.

"And there before me was a second beast, which looked like a bear. It was raised up on one of its sides, and it had three ribs in its mouth between its teeth. It was told, 'Get up and eat your fill of flesh!'

"After that, I looked, and there before me was another beast, one that looked like a leopard. And on its back it had four wings like those of a bird. This beast had four heads, and it was given authority to rule.

"After that, in my vision at night I looked, and there before me was a fourth beast—terrifying and frightening and very powerful. It had large iron teeth; it crushed and devoured its victims and trampled underfoot whatever was left. It was different from all the former beasts, and it had ten horns.

"While I was thinking about the horns, there before me was another horn, a little one, which came up among them; and three of the first horns were uprooted before it. This horn had eyes like the eyes of a man and a mouth that spoke boastfully.

"As I looked,

"thrones were set in place,
       and the Ancient of Days took his seat.
His clothing was as white as snow;
       the hair of his head was white like wool.
His throne was flaming with fire,
       and its wheels were all ablaze.
A river of fire was flowing,
       coming out from before him.
Thousands upon thousands attended him;
       ten thousand times ten thousand stood before him.
The court was seated,
       and the books were opened.

"Then I continued to watch because of the boastful words the horn was speaking. I kept looking until the beast was slain and its body destroyed and thrown into the blazing fire. (The other beasts had been stripped of their authority, but were allowed to live for a period of time.)"

Barbara Tuchman is a contemporary historian whose works on neglected periods of history have been unusually popular. Her secret, she explains, is writing "history by the ounce." That is, instead of fitting her books with long lists of dates that most of us find quite dull, she packs her pages with punchy anecdotes that capture far more of the spirit of the period than can be done by any mere listing of facts. History by the ounce! That is a good way to describe Daniel's preview of gentile history as presented in the seventh chapter of his prophecy. The time frame is extensive—from the sixth century B.C. until the coming of Jesus Christ and beyond. But Daniel packs it all in through a series of vivid visions that convey far more than any mere listing of names, battles, or dates could do for us.

The material in this section is parallel to the vision of Nebuchadnezzar recorded in chapter 2, but it is important to see that an entirely new section of the book begins with chapter 7. For one thing, the first six chapters have presented the career of Daniel in chronological order through a series of three kings under whom Daniel served: Nebuchadnezzar, Belshazzar, and Darius. Now the account skips backward to something that happened in the reign of the second of these kings. Moreover, the nature of the material changes. The first chapters contain historical events from Daniel's years of service. True, there is the record of the dream of Nebuchadnezzar, but even this is set in the context of the threat it posed to Daniel and his three friends, and the story involves his success in interpreting it. The second half of the book (chapters 7–12) is trans-historical. It is a record of visions that could have been received and recorded at any period of history either before or after Daniel's time.

These visions vary in important details, but they are overlapping and make roughly the same points. They tell us that God is in control of history, that human kingdoms will succeed human kingdoms until the coming of the Lord's Anointed, the Messiah, but that in the end it is his kingdom that will fill the whole earth.

The Vision of Four Beasts

The first vision of Daniel 7 is the foundation for what follows. So it is important to have it firmly in mind as we proceed. Daniel saw four wild animals that later we are told represent "four kingdoms that will rise from the earth" (v. 17). The first was like a lion, although it had eagle's wings. It had its wings torn off and then was lifted up from the ground so that it stood on two feet. Daniel says that the heart of a man was given to it. The second animal looked like a bear. The distinguishing feature of this animal was that it had three ribs in its mouth and that it was told, "Get up and eat your fill of flesh." The third animal was like a leopard, but it had four wings like the wings of a bird. It also had four heads and was given authority to rule. The fourth beast was the most terrifying of all. It is not even compared to a known animal. Daniel says only that it had large iron teeth and ten horns. It crushed and devoured its victims and trampled everything underfoot.

While Daniel was thinking about this last beast, particularly about the significance of the ten horns, another horn appeared that uprooted three of the beast's ten horns. This last horn is said to have had eyes like the eyes of a man and a mouth that spoke boastfully.

At this point a judgment unfolded. Thrones were set up in heaven, and the Ancient of Days took his seat. The Ancient of Days is God. Thousands worshiped him. The court convened, the books were opened, and the beasts were judged, particularly the last one whose body was destroyed and thrown into a river of fire that flowed from God's throne. The vision ends by the statement that "one like a son of man" approached the Ancient of Days and was given "authority, glory and sovereign power." "All peoples, nations and men of every language worshiped him. His dominion is an everlasting dominion that will not pass away, and his kingdom is one that will never be destroyed" (vv. 13–14).

The most obvious thing to be said about this vision is that it is parallel to Nebuchadnezzar's dream of the great statue made up of various kinds of metals—although this vision adds significant new details.

The beast that was like a lion corresponds to the golden portion of Nebuchadnezzar's statue: the head. This was a representation of the Babylonian empire itself, as Daniel explained to the emperor (Dan. 2:26–28). However, in this second vision details are added that seem particularly apt as a description of Nebuchadnezzar himself. In view of what we have already been told about Nebuchadnezzar, the tearing off of the animal's wings seems to symbolize Nebuchadnezzar's humbling and the reducing of his glory during the years of his insanity. When it is said that the lion-like animal was raised up on two feet and given the heart of a man, it is hard not to think of the restoration of the proud king's reason. These details help fix our earlier interpretation of the first vision and establish a pattern for understanding the parts of the vision that follow.

The second animal, which was like a bear, corresponds to the silver portions of the statue: the arms, shoulders, and upper parts of the body. This represents the kingdom of the Medes and Persians. Incidentally, it also shows that these two kingdoms are to be taken together, not divided as has been done by the more liberal scholars.[1] Nothing in the history of the Median Empire corresponds to the detail of the three ribs held between the second beast's teeth. But if the kingdom is that of the Medes and Persians (considered together), then the history fits quite well. Cyrus, the Median-Persian king, and his son Cambyses conquered (1) the Lydian kingdom in Asia Minor, which fell to Cyrus in 546 B.C.; (2) the Chaldean Empire, which he overthrew in 539 B.C.; and (3) the kingdom of Egypt, which fell to Cambyses in 525.

The third beast corresponds to the middle portion of Nebuchadnezzar's statue, the part made of bronze, and represents the Greek Empire of Alexander the Great. Two things particularly characterized this empire: the speed with which it was achieved and the speed with which it divided into four separate kingdoms after its founder's death. Like a swiftly running leopard, Alexander won his vast empire in one extended campaign. But within a few years of his death in 323 B.C., the kingdom fractured into four parts: (1) the region of Greece and Macedonia under Antipater, (2) Thrace and Asia Minor under Lysimachus, (3) Asia (except Asia Minor and Palestine) under Seleucus, and (4) Egypt and Palestine under Ptolemy.

There is no way this fourfold division can be projected onto the Persian Empire, as the liberal view must do to be consistent. The Persian Empire remained intact until its sudden collapse to Alexander in 334–332 B.C.[2]

The final beast of Daniel's dream, the terrible one unlike any known animal, corresponds to the legs, feet, and toes of Nebuchadnezzar's statue and represents Rome. Several details of the visions tie the statue and beast together. The legs of the statue are iron; so are the teeth of the animal. The animal has ten horns; these find a parallel in the ten toes of the statue, presumably representing ten confederated kingdoms. However, a new feature is introduced in the vision of the four beasts that was not present in the vision of the statue: the appearance of "another horn, a little one," which replaced three of the horns of the last and terrible beast. The horns (and toes) would seem to be kingdoms. But this horn has characteristics of an individual ruler. This seems to be the first biblical reference to the individual later described in the Bible as the Antichrist. He appears in 2 Thessalonians 2 as "the man of lawlessness . . . doomed for destruction" (v. 3) and is seen again in Revelation.

At this point, we are reminded of the stone uncut by human hands that came and struck the great statue of Nebuchadnezzar so that it fell and was broken in pieces and then was scattered by the wind. The stone then grew to become a great mountain that filled the earth. In this second vision the judgment of God is passed upon the world's kingdom, and all "authority, glory and sovereign power" are given to the "son of man," whom we recognize as Jesus.

This last part of the vision is so important that we must consider it by itself in the next chapter.

Man's View, God's View

I wrote a moment ago that the most obvious point to be made about the vision of the four beasts is that it parallels the vision of the statue, and this is true. But it is also obvious that although the two accounts are parallel, they are nevertheless not presented from the same perspective. On the contrary, the perspectives are radically different. In the first the outlook is quite human, the way a man or woman might look at these great empires. In the second the perspective is God's. It tells us how God views the world's kingdoms.

How does man view the world's kingdoms? Well, he is impressed, for the most part. He thinks of them as glorious—differing in splendor, to be sure, but nevertheless all worthy of some degree of honor. He is enamored of them. On occasion he is seduced by the secular political power. He sees the state as the greatest of all good and as an end in itself.

How does God view earth's kingdoms? A mixed answer must be given at this point. It is mixed because, on the one hand, God has created and authorized the secular authorities, as Romans 13 indicates ("The authorities that exist have been established by God. Consequently, he who rebels against the authority is rebelling against what God has instituted, and those who do so will bring judgment on themselves" [vv. 1–2]). But on the other hand, the state is generally corrupt and therefore aptly described as beastlike, which is what the vision of beasts in Daniel 7 does.

From God's point of view the state is not so much a noble, glorious thing as it is an animal that conquers, devours, and tears those subject to it. What is more characteristic of the kingdoms of this world's history: the properly functioning state of Romans 13 or the corrupt, devouring state of Revelation 13? It would be nice if we could point confidently to Romans 13. Unfortunately, honesty compels us to admit that the kingdoms of this world have often been terrible and ferocious and richly deserve judgment.

By comparing the vision of Nebuchadnezzar in Daniel 2 and the vision of Daniel in Daniel 7, we must also admit that the latter is the way God seems most often to view them.

Who Rules History?

Not only does the vision of the four beasts indicate how God regards the supposedly glorious kingdoms of this world. It also reveals a glimpse of that kingdom which truly is glorious, in whose light all the imagined achievements of men and movements of history are to be evaluated. In this area the visions convey several important ideas.

1. *God rules in history.* This is an obvious point and one that has already been seen several times in Daniel. Indeed, it is the chief message of the book. When Nebuchadnezzar set up his great golden statue in the plain of Dura, he did so in defiance of God who had said that Nebuchadnezzar's kingdom would pass away and be succeeded by another, even though it was glorious enough in human terms to be described as a head of gold. Nebuchadnezzar said in effect, "My kingdom is an everlasting dominion that will never be destroyed" (cf. Dan. 7:14). But his kingdom *was* destroyed—by Cyrus the Persian—because it is the decree of God and not the desire of man that rules history. In Daniel 5, when Belshazzar at his great feast defiled the vessels of God taken from the temple in Jerusalem, he too was saying, "I determine my own history." But he was wrong! God numbered his days and brought them to an end. God weighed him and declared that he was found wanting. God divided his kingdom, giving it to the Medes and Persians. This is the point made in Daniel's vision. The bestial empires of world history may roar and frighten for a time. They may crush kingdoms weaker than they are. But in the end, all will be brought to judgment and the kingdom of God's Anointed alone will be established. This is because God, and not mere human beings, is in charge.

You must apply this personally. If you are in a position of power and influence, you are in danger of thinking that the power you exercise somehow flows from you because of the exceptional person you are. If you are wealthy, you are in danger of thinking that your wealth is self-generated—that you are wealthy because you are better than other people. The same danger exists if you are good-looking or have a natural way with people or a talent that is in much demand.

None of these things comes from yourself. Rather, all are God's gift to you, and he can both give them and take them away. He can raise a person up, and he can bring that one down. He does! He does it constantly.

The truth that God rules history may also be applied in a comforting way. I think of that section of our Lord's sermon on the Mount of Olives shortly before his arrest and crucifixion in which he gave his disciples a forecast of things to come. There will be many false christs ("antichrists") who will deceive many, he said. There will be wars and rumors of wars. There will be widespread apostasy as many turn from the faith. People will hate and betray one another. Wickedness will increase. Indeed, at the very end "the abomination that causes desolation"—a clear reference to Daniel 9:27, 11:31, and 12:11—will appear. It will usher in a time of "great distress, unequaled from the beginning of the world until now—and never to be equaled again" (Matt. 24:21). Still, in spite of this great turmoil that will cause the hearts of many to shake with fear, Christ's words to his disciples are words of comfort. "See to it that you are not alarmed. Such things must happen, but the end is still to come" (v. 6).

How is it that Jesus can tell his own not to be alarmed in such circumstances? False christs? Wars? Apostasy? Hatred? Betrayal? Wickedness? How can we not be troubled so long as we have hearts to feel and minds to grieve with those who are suffering? The answer—the only possible answer—is that, in spite of these things, God is in control of history and will yet work all things out in accordance with his just and all-wise plan for humanity. As Daniel shows, in the end the wicked will be judged and the saints will reign with Jesus.

2. *The kingdom of Jesus Christ will triumph over the kingdoms of this world and will endure forever.* This idea was present in the vision of the statue given to Nebuchadnezzar, for in that vision a rock not made with human hands struck the statue and destroyed it, after which it grew to be a large mountain that filled the earth. But there is a new element here, and that is the personal rule of God's Anointed, described as being "like a son of man."

We are going to consider this further in the next chapter, but it is important to note that this is the very phrase picked up by Jesus and used over and over as a title for himself. Indeed, he used it in the Olivet discourse just a few verses after his reference to Daniel, saying, "For as lightning that comes from the east is visible even in the west, so will be the coming of the Son of Man" (Matt. 24:27). There are other references to the coming of this Son of Man in Daniel's prophecy.

3. *The saints of the Most High will reign with Jesus.* In the interpretation of this vision in the latter half of Daniel 7, it is said that the saints will be persecuted by the king who is the little horn (vv. 24–25); but he will be destroyed, and the "sovereignty, power and greatness of the kingdoms under the whole heaven will be handed over to the saints, the people of the Most High" (v. 27). To my knowledge this is the first occurrence of this idea in the Bible—that the saints will rule with Jesus and not merely that Jesus will himself reign. It is an astonishing truth, but a very practical one.

One practical application is made by Paul in 1 Corinthians 6:1–11. In those verses Paul is concerned with the practice of the Corinthian Christians of going to law against one another. He argues, "Do you not know that the saints will judge the world? And if you are to judge the world, are you not competent to judge trivial cases?" (v. 2). It is a powerful argument. If we are to rule with the Lord Jesus Christ one day, we should be able to show something of the wisdom and justice of his rule now—and not have to appeal to unbelievers to settle our internal disputes. More than that, we should be models of integrity, compassion, love, honesty, and wisdom in our dealings with other men and women.

There is this application also. In 2 Timothy 2:12, Paul says, "If we endure, we will also reign with him." The context has to do with our remaining faithful to the Lord in difficult times. So it is in the nature of a warning as well as an encouragement. We can be encouraged to endure now because we know that one day we will reign with Jesus. That can lift our spirits and give us a renewed determination to fight on. It is also a warning since our reigning with Christ later seems to depend on our endurance now. It is the same thing Jesus meant when he said, "Because of the increase of wickedness, the love of most will grow cold, but he who stands firm to the end will be saved" (Matt. 24:12–13). Are you enduring? Will you be standing firm when Christ returns?

You may ague that this is a tough age in which to be faithful, and that is true. But it was tough for Daniel; the empires were in political and moral decline in his day. And it was tough for Paul, who makes these applications for us; the Roman Empire of the first Christian century was particularly decadent. It has always been tough for God's people. But those who truly are his people persevere—as they look forward to Christ's reign and to reigning with him.

10

A Vision of Jesus Christ

Daniel 7:13-14

In my vision at night I looked, and there before me was one like a son of man, coming with the clouds of heaven. He approached the Ancient of Days and was led into his presence. He was given authority, glory and sovereign power; all peoples, nations and men of every language worshiped him. His dominion is an everlasting dominion that will not pass away, and his kingdom is one that will never be destroyed.

In the midst of the seventh chapter of Daniel, which records Daniel's vision of the four beasts representing four successive human governments, there are two verses that I find fascinating. They are a record of a vision Daniel had of the Lord Jesus Christ, and they are fascinating because they are unique in the Old Testament. The verses before these show how the kingdoms of the world will be judged. But at the peak of the vision, at the very point at which we might expect the rule of God the Father himself to be affirmed, we read, "I looked, and there before me was one like a son of man, coming with the clouds of heaven. He approached the Ancient of Days and was led into his presence. *He* was given authority, glory and sovereign power; all peoples, nations and men of every language worshiped *him*. *His* dominion is an everlasting dominion that will not pass away, and *his* kingdom is one that will never be destroyed" (vv. 13–14).

This is an unusual and fascinating passage because it presents a vision of Jesus that is not found elsewhere in the Old Testament.

The Old Testament Witness

When I say this I do not imply that there are no other prophecies in the Old Testament that concern Jesus, for that is not true. Indeed, not only are there clear prophecies of Christ, there are also intimations of a plurality within the Godhead and even of the possible appearance of Jesus on earth in a pre-incarnate form.

The first intimation of a plurality in the Godhead is in the first verse of the Bible where the plural name for God, *Elohim*, occurs. Students of Hebrew rightly point out that this does not necessarily imply the existence of more than one God or of a number of persons within the Godhead. It can be a plural of emphasis, as if it meant "the God of all gods." But later in the same chapter we find this one true God saying, "Let *us* make man in *our* image, in *our* likeness" (Gen. 1:26). And later, at Babel we find God saying, "Come, let *us* go down and confuse their language so they will not understand each other" (Gen. 11:7). There are verses like that scattered throughout the Old Testament.

As I say, the use of a plural name for God does not necessarily imply a plurality of persons within the Godhead. But it is not just the name of God that is plural. God is referred to by plural pronouns also, and this is strange in a book that stresses the truth that there is only one God—unless it is meant to indicate a plurality in God that is, as we know, increasingly disclosed in the Bible anyway.

Another intimation of the existence of a second person in the Godhead is the appearance of a figure who is usually described as "the angel of the Lord" or "the messenger of the Lord." The first clear reference to this figure is God's appearance to Abraham to warn him of the destruction of Sodom and Gomorrah. In that story three figures appear to Abraham. Two may be angels. But the third, who does most of the talking and who speaks to Abraham as God, saying, "Shall I hide from Abraham what I am about to do?" (Gen. 18:17), seems more than an angel. He speaks as only God can speak, and the chapter probably refers to him at the very beginning where we read, "The LORD appeared to Abraham near the great tree of Mamre while he was sitting at the entrance to his tent" (v. 1).

God may have appeared as this figure to Adam and Eve in the garden in the cool of the day.

This is probably also the figure seen in chapter 3 of Daniel. In that chapter one "like a son of the gods" appeared with Shadrach, Meshach, and Abednego in the midst of the blazing furnace and protected them. He was even seen by the unbelieving Nebuchadnezzar.

I refer to one more Old Testament passage. In the sixth chapter of Isaiah that great prophet writes, "In the year that King Uzziah died, I saw the Lord seated on a throne, high and exalted, and the train of his robe filled the temple" (v. 1). In itself this would hardly be remarkable. But in John 12:41, the fourth evangelist says that Isaiah "saw Jesus' glory and spoke about him," presumably referring to this vision. In other words, in John's view Isaiah saw Jesus seated as God in the heavenly temple.

These and other texts hint, often in stimulating ways, of the existence of the second person of the Trinity. Yet they are sometimes unclear, and they are certainly subject to differing interpretations. Nowhere but in Daniel 7:13–14 (except perhaps in Psalm 110:1) does the distinct person and glory of the Lord Jesus Christ emerge so clearly. For here are two great personages: The Ancient of Days and "one like a son of man." And it is to this latter figure that dominion over the peoples and nations of the earth is given forever.

The Theme of Daniel

Unusual and unexpected as Daniel's vision of the Lord Jesus Christ in the Old Testament is, it is actually precisely what we should expect at this point in Daniel's prophecy. Indeed, it is the high point of the book thus far.

What is the theme of Daniel? We saw it at the very beginning when we read that Nebuchadnezzar took the holy articles from the temple of God in Jerusalem and carried them back to Babylon, where he laid them up in the temple of his god. It was a way of declaring that, in Nebuchadnezzar's judgment, the gods of Babylon were superior to and more powerful than the Jewish God, Jehovah.

But were they? It seemed so. Jerusalem had fallen to Nebuchadnezzar's armies. However, the entire development of the book shows that God's answer to the question is that God is still in control of history—although the kingdom of Babylon had triumphed for a time. As a result, the kingdom of Nebuchadnezzar would eventually fall to the kingdom of the Medes and Persians under Darius; the kingdom of Darius would eventually fall to the kingdom of the Greeks under Alexander the Great; the Greek kingdom would fall to the Romans. And only at the end of that long history, which God was controlling, would there come an eternal kingdom that, like a rock, would destroy the other kingdoms, grow to be a great mountain, and fill the earth.

How can any mere human kingdom, however blessed by God, take on these eternal characteristics? When God told David that he would establish his kingdom forever, David understood this difficulty and protested rightly, "Is this your usual way of dealing with man, O Sovereign LORD?" (2 Sam. 7:19).

David meant that human kingdoms do not endure forever. How then can any kingdom grow to be a great mountain?

The answer comes in Daniel 7:13–14. The one who is to establish and maintain this kingdom, while he is "like a son of man," that is, a human being, is no mere human being, and his kingdom is no mere human kingdom. The one who is "like a son of man" is also God; he is the God-man. And his kingdom is to be established by God in spite of the rebellious opposition of Nebuchadnezzar, Belshazzar, or any other of this world's emperors.

Jesus, the Son of Man

To my mind, the most interesting thing of all is the way Jesus referred to Daniel 7:13–14 in his teachings and applied the title "Son of Man" to himself. There are many titles for Jesus in the New Testament. He is the "Lord," "Christ" (Messiah), the "Good Shepherd," the "bridegroom." He is "the Alpha and Omega, the beginning and the end." He is "the first and the last." Many titles of God the Father are given to him. He is the great "I Am." But Jesus never used these titles for himself. Others gave them to him. He did not even use the word "Messiah," except on one occasion when he was speaking to the Samaritan woman (John 4:26). The only biblical title that Jesus did use, and that almost exclusively, was the title "Son of Man," which he got from Daniel. It is used sixty-nine times in the Synoptics and twelve times in John.

This has fascinated scholars. One of the most useful books I have read on the Jewish expectations of the Messiah is by the great Norwegian scholar Sigmund Mowinckel, entitled *He That Cometh*.[1] This is a major study running to more than five hundred pages, but it devotes one hundred of these pages to a study of Jesus' use of the words "Son of Man." This is because it was Jesus' own term for himself, as I indicated, and also because Mowinckel wanted to answer the question why Jesus used this term rather than one of the other much more common and more readily understood titles. According to Mowinckel, there are two reasons Jesus used it.

First, it was an ideal title for combining the two chief things that needed to be said about his person: namely, that he was fully man and that at the same time he was fully God.

The truth that he was fully man is conveyed by the term itself, for the words "son of man" in Aramaic or Hebrew idiom simply mean "man" or "a human being." For example, if an Aramaic- or Hebrew-speaking person wanted to refer to a person as a sinner, it would be natural for him to speak of that one as a "son of sin." Or similarly, if he wanted to call a person wealthy, he might have referred to him as a "son of wealth." When our Lord referred to himself as a "Son of Man," he was merely calling himself a man, so far as the literal meaning of the term goes. That alone is significant, for it reveals the delight the Lord Jesus Christ, the eternal Son of God, had in identifying with us. He could have used terms that stressed his deity, but instead he stressed his humanity. It is as if he were saying, "I am one of you, and I am happy with that identification."

But there is more to it than this. For Jesus did not merely refer to himself as "*a* son of man," which would have expressed only his humanity. He referred to himself as "the Son of Man," which means "the son of man referred to in Daniel"—that is, the son of man who came on the clouds of heaven and to whom the Ancient of Days gave authority, glory, and sovereign power. He did this at his trial. When asked by Caiaphas whether he was "Christ, the Son of God," Jesus replied, "Yes, it is as you say. . . . But I say to all of you: In the future you will see the Son of Man sitting at the right hand of the Mighty One and coming on the clouds of heaven" (Matt. 26:64). This is a clear reference to Daniel 7:13–14. It is a way of saying, "I am the divine King prophesied by Daniel." And, of course, this is precisely how the Jewish rulers understood it. For after he had said this, Caiaphas cried out, "He has spoken blasphemy! Why do we need any more witnesses?" (v. 65), and they condemned him to death.

The second reason Jesus used the title "Son of Man" rather than one of the other more familiar and more explicit messianic titles current in Judaism, according to Mowinckel—the chief reason in his opinion—is precisely because it was less explicit and because Jesus could then infuse it with his own meaning instead of picking up on the earnest but nevertheless very wrong expectations of his contemporaries.

There were tremendous expectations of a messianic deliverer in Christ's day. The country was under Rome's rule, and all patriotic Jews earnestly waited for the deliverer who had been prophesied in the Old Testament. Who was he? Whenever anybody the least bit above average came along, there were always hundreds and even thousands of people who were ready to look to him and follow him in hopes he might be the one expected. They even had a certain checklist of questions they would ask such charismatic figures. John the Baptist was asked this list of questions (John 1:19–28). He had a dramatic and effective ministry. So the authorities sent a delegation to ask him whether he was the Messiah.

"I am not the Christ," he answered.

"Are you Elijah then?" They knew that Malachi, the last book of the Old Testament, had prophesied that Elijah would come as Christ's forerunner (Mal. 4:5).

"I am not," John responded.

There was only one other messianic-type figure they could think of, and that was the "prophet" mentioned by Moses in Deuteronomy 18:15, 18. "Are you the Prophet?" they asked.

Again John said, "No" (cf. John 1:19–21). That exhausted their questions, and they went back to the authorities in Jerusalem with their report. They did not give much attention to John's claim to be the "voice of one calling in the desert, 'Make straight the way for the Lord'" (John 1:23), and they certainly did not believe him when he identified Jesus of Nazareth as the one whose way he had prepared. The incident shows how intense the Jewish expectations for a political deliverer were at this time. If Jesus had said, "Yes, I am the Messiah," or if he had used any one of the other titles usually identified with this figure, the Jews would have thought of him in simple political terms. And they would have followed him in the belief that he was a mere man, like David, whom God had sent to drive out the Romans and restore the Davidic throne.

By rejecting these titles and instead choosing the less explicit but intriguing title "Son of Man," Jesus was able to identify himself in his own way and avoid misunderstandings.

The important questions are: How did Jesus interpret this title? What meaning did he give to the figure of the Son of Man in Daniel? There are several teachings.

1. *He used it to teach his pre-existence.* In John 3:13, just a few verses before John 3:36, Jesus said of himself, "No one has ever gone into heaven except the one who came from heaven—the Son of Man." I am sure that even the disciples, who were often slow to understand the Lord's teaching, would have recognized this statement as a reference to Daniel. They would have perceived Jesus to be teaching that he was the same figure seen by the prophet so many years before. In John 6:62 there is a similar passage. There Jesus asks, "What if you see the Son of Man ascend to where he was before!" That is, before he came to earth Jesus was seated at the right hand of God the Father in heaven. What if he should abandon his work on earth because of human unbelief and return there?

The existence of Jesus is not determined from the date of his incarnation. Our existence is determined from the date of our birth. That is why we celebrate birthdays. Before that we were not; now we are. This is not the case with Jesus Christ. There was a date at which he was born of the Virgin Mary, but this is not the point at which the existence of Jesus started. He existed before that, even before the point at which the prophet Daniel saw him. Being God, he existed from eternity.

2. *He used it to teach that he must suffer.* Nothing in Daniel 7:13–14 teaches that the Messiah must suffer, though Daniel 9:26 suggests it. But Jesus always understood and taught that this was the role he was to fill. A moment ago I referred to John 3:13, which teaches the Son of Man's pre-existence. The very next verse uses the title again, but this time in reference to his death on the cross. "Just as Moses lifted up the snake in the desert, so the Son of Man must be lifted up, that everyone who believes in him may have eternal life" (John 3:14–15).

This was the hardest thing Jesus had to get across, but it was because his contemporaries were thinking of a political messiah. They wanted a hero, not a Savior who was to be crucified on a cross. If Jesus had described himself as the Messiah, that is all they ever would have thought. Instead he called himself the Son of Man and taught that he must first suffer and die for our salvation.

3. *He used it to teach that a person must be personally joined to him to be saved.* "Unless you eat the flesh of the Son of Man and drink his blood, you have no life in you. Whoever eats my flesh and drinks my blood has eternal life, and I will raise him up at the last day" (John 6:53–54). As the chapter proceeds, it is clear that "eating and drinking" is a metaphor for faith. To be saved a person must believe on Jesus, and that belief is a thing that makes Christ as much a part of the believer as a literal eating or drinking of him would do.

4. *He used it to teach about the final judgment.* "A time is coming and has now come when the dead will hear the voice of the Son of God and those who hear will live. For as the Father has life in himself, so he has granted the Son to have

life in himself. And he has given him authority to judge because he is the Son of Man" (John 5:25–27). This is another reference to Daniel as Jesus' use of the words "authority" and "because he is the Son of Man" makes clear. In Daniel the one like a son of man participates with the Ancient of Days in his judgment, and it is as a consequence of that judgment that "authority, glory and sovereign power" are given to him. Jesus claims to be judge of all men because he is the Son of Man. In the days of his flesh he was the gentle Jesus who surrendered himself to death for our salvation. But the day is coming when he shall return as the glorified and reigning Lord, and in that day he will judge all people on the basis of their relationship to him. Are they subjects of his kingdom? Do they bow before him and welcome his rule? Or are they rebels who have resisted his rightful sovereignty over them, whom he will judge?

All Shall Bow

One day every knee will bow before the rightful authority of Jesus Christ. It is what Daniel says: "All peoples, nations and men of every language worshiped him" (Dan. 7:14). Paul says the same, arguing, "God exalted him to the highest place and gave him the name that is above every name, that at the name of Jesus every knee should bow, in heaven and on earth and under the earth, and every tongue confess that Jesus Christ is Lord, to the glory of God the Father" (Phil. 2:9–11). That is a large number of people—"all peoples, nations and men of every language" and *every* knee . . . in heaven and on earth and under the earth."

The Bible says that *all* will worship and that *every* knee will bow. You will bow. But will it be willingly as you kneel to adore the One who gave his life to purchase your salvation? Or will you bow reluctantly as you are forced to your knees by one of his glorious angels just moments before you are judged for your sin and banished forever from his holy and blessed presence? If it is to be a willing adoration, it must be adoration now. You must believe on him now. Then you will be part of that heavenly company described as "numbering thousands upon thousands, and ten thousand times ten thousand" who will encircle the throne of God saying,

> Worthy is the Lamb, who was slain,
> to receive power and wealth and wisdom and strength
> and honor and glory and praise!

and who sing together with every living creature,

> To him who sits on the throne and to the Lamb
> be praise and honor and glory and power,
>   for ever and ever!

>   Revelation 5:11–13

11

End of an Era

Daniel 8:1-27

He said: "I am going to tell you what will happen later in the time of wrath, because the vision concerns the appointed time of the end. The two-horned ram that you saw represents the kings of Media and Persia. The shaggy goat is the king of Greece, and the large horn between his eyes is the first king. The four horns that replaced the one that was broken off represent four kingdoms that will emerge from his nation but will not have the same power.

"In the latter part of their reign, when rebels have become completely wicked, a stern-faced king, a master of intrigue, will arise. He will become very strong, but not by his own power. He will cause astounding devastation and will succeed in whatever he does. He will destroy the mighty men and the holy people. He will cause deceit to prosper, and he will consider himself superior. When they feel secure, he will destroy many and take his stand against the Prince of princes. Yet he will be destroyed, but not by human power.

"The vision of the evenings and mornings that has been given you is true, but seal up the vision, for it concerns the distant future."

When I first began to preach through Daniel, one of the elders of Tenth Presbyterian Church asked me, "Are you going to do the second half of the book?" Normally that would be a strange question, since a book study involves the whole book and because it is my practice to preach through whole books of the Bible systematically. But in this case the question was not strange. The first and second halves of Daniel are quite different, and in the minds of many the value of a slow study of the second part is doubtful.

88

Why? It is because the first half is narrative and the second half is prophecy. True, there is some overlap. The first half also contains prophecy, as in the case of Nebuchadnezzar's vision of the great statue composed of different types of metals. The second half also has narrative elements. Still, the value of the first half is in its account of the way in which Daniel and his three friends functioned in pagan Babylon and how God protected them in the midst of that hostile pagan environment. The second half focuses on prophecies of the end times; and not only do we not always see clearly how they relate to us, we do not even fully understand them. How can we relate to visions of animals that represent nations and kingdoms? And what are we to think of little horns that rise up to destroy other horns? We wonder if any of this can be practical.

Well, it is difficult to understand and apply some of these things. But what I hope to show is that the symbolic elements of these visions are not all equally difficult to interpret and that there are practical lessons in them.

A Shift in Emphasis

Daniel 8 contains a vision of a ram and a goat, which gives additional detail about a period of history that has been described twice already. The initial vision of the statue of various kinds of metals, which Nebuchadnezzar had and which is recorded in chapter 2, spoke of four successive world empires: the empire of Babylon ruled by Nebuchadnezzar, the kingdom of the Medes and Persians that followed it, the Greek Empire established by Alexander the Great, and the final, powerful empire of Rome. The vision we now have, the vision of the ram and goat, corresponds to the second and third parts of that initial vision. That is, the ram represents the Median-Persian Empire; that is why it is described as having two horns, each horn representing one-half of that empire. One horn is described as being longer or more powerful than the other, just as one side of the bear was described as being higher. This corresponds to the dominance of the Persian element in the two-nation coalition.

Similarly, the goat represents the kingdom of the Greeks under Alexander. The goat has one horn, which represents Alexander himself. It is described as "crossing the whole earth without touching the ground" (Dan. 8:5), that is, crossing it quickly, as Alexander did in his remarkable three-year conquest of the entire Persian Empire. The elaboration of this vision shows that the great horn was suddenly broken off and that four other horns replaced it, which is what happened. Alexander died suddenly at the age of thirty-three, and his empire was divided into four parts under Ptolemy, Seleucus, Lysimachus, and Cassander. In other words, the vision of chapter 8 focuses on the middle portions of the vision of chapter 2 and gives additional details.

The same thing is true when we compare this vision with the four unusual animals of chapter 7. Those were (1) a beast like a lion, representing Babylon; (2) a beast like a bear, representing the Medes and Persians; (3) a beast like a leopard, representing Greece; and (4) a beast unlike any known animal, representing Rome. The ram corresponds to the bear. The goat corresponds to the leopard.

Why is this new vision given? Is it just to add details? Or is there a shift in emphasis or a new purpose? An important clue to Daniel's purpose in this vision is the fact that the language in which he is writing changes from Aramaic to Hebrew at this point. The opening part of Daniel is in Hebrew, from the first verse of chapter 1 through the third verse of chapter 2. But from Daniel 2:4 through the end of chapter 7 everything has been written in Aramaic.

Now this changes, as I said. Chapter 8 switches to Hebrew, and this is the language used through the very end of Daniel. This is unparalleled in any other biblical book, and the only explanation I can think of is that Daniel wrote in the language of the people to whom he primarily wanted these various parts of the book to be directed. Chapters 2–7 concern the predicted flow of the various gentile world empires and concern the gentile world especially. So they are written in Aramaic, the dominant gentile language of that day. By contrast, chapters 8–12, which are written in Hebrew, chiefly concern the Jews.

What we are going to see is that these chapters deal with a particular era in Jewish history. Indeed, they predict the end of this era and thus anticipate a new era of gentile (and Jewish) blessing.

A Second "Little Horn"

The chief new element of this vision and the part that particularly concerned the Jews in this period is the prediction of another "little horn" who would desecrate the sanctuary and persecute the people of the "Beautiful Land." I say *another* little horn, because it would be a mistake to confuse this individual with the little horn in chapter 7. Some have done this, but a careful comparison of the two chapters shows that this is wrong. The little horn of chapter 7 is connected with the fourth of the four kingdoms, Rome.

There are difficulties in interpreting this part of Daniel, as we will see. However this little horn is to be interpreted, it is at least clear that he arises from the Roman Empire. Daniel describes the Roman Empire as existing in ten related kingdoms, represented by the ten toes of Nebuchadnezzar's statue or the ten horns of the fourth terrible beast of Daniel 7. The little horn of chapter 7 uproots and replaces three of these horns. By contrast, the little horn of chapter 8 rises from the kingdom of Greece. He does not replace the other rulers. He merely arises from them in due course (v. 9). His destructive energies are directed against the Jewish people and their sanctuary.

There can be little doubt that this is a prophecy of the career of the Greek king Antiochus IV Epiphanes who was one of the greatest enemies of the Jewish people in all history.

Antiochus IV was the eighth king of the Seleucid dynasty, which was itself one of the four powers into which the Greek Empire was divided after the death of Alexander. Daniel describes him as being "wicked" and "a master of intrigue" (v. 23), and this is exactly what he was. He began by usurping the throne from his nephew, the son of his older brother Seleucis IV, and immediately after that he launched a campaign of ruthless conquest in the Near East. In 170/169 B.C. he invaded Egypt. In Jerusalem he tried to impose religious and cultural uniformity by suppressing Jewish worship. Already in 175 B.C., at the beginning of his reign, he had expelled the godly high priest Onias III and had replaced him with Onias's hellenizing younger brother Jason. He put an end to the daily sacrifices at the temple, forbade the circumcision of Jewish infants, and made it a crime to possess a copy of the Jewish Scriptures.

All this came to a head in December 168 B.C. when Antiochus seized Jerusalem by treachery. He had been turned back from Alexandria by the Roman commander Popilius Laenas and now took out his frustration in a bitter and repressive campaign against Jews. He sent his general Apollonius into the city with 20,000 troops and there erected an idol of Zeus in the temple area. He desecrated the altar by offering swine upon it. This was the greatest affront to faithful Judaism that could possibly be imagined, and the idol became known to the Jews as "the abomination of desolation" (cf. Dan. 11:31) and later served as a type of that future abomination to be caused by the Antichrist in the last days (cf. Matt. 24:15).

Daniel says that this little horn would "consider himself superior" (Dan. 8:25), and this was certainly true of Antiochus. His name comes from the inscription he had minted on coins of the time that bore his image: THEOS EPIPHANES ("God made manifest"). During the reign of this man pious Jews experienced a time of unparalleled suffering.

Twenty-Three Hundred Days

A puzzle in this vision is the time element of 2,300 evenings and mornings that Daniel introduces in verse 14. Here an angel or holy one is speaking, and he says, "It will take 2,300 evenings and mornings; then the sanctuary will be reconsecrated." This defines the duration of the time of persecution.

Generally this has been interpreted in one of two ways. Either it is seen as referring to 2,300 twenty-four-hour days, that is, six years and 111 days, or it is seen as referring to 1,150 days and 1,150 evenings, which reduces the time to half, that is, to three years and 55 days. I do not need to present the evidence of both sides of this division, but I refer to Gleason Archer who feels that the preponderance of evidence "favor[s] the latter interpretation."[1] The argument is not so much linguistic here as historical. The temple was reconsecrated by Judas Maccabaeus on December 14, 164 B.C., and it appears that Antiochus IV Epiphanes began his repression of Jewish worship about three years, rather than six years, earlier. (It is hard to be precise because we do not know the specific acts of desecration that may have been involved.)

There is one additional detail that is also worth noting. Daniel predicts the end of Antiochus, but not by human hands, saying, "He will be destroyed, but not by human power" (v. 25). That is not what might naturally be expected. We might expect that his successor, Judas Maccabaeus, should have unseated and killed him. But in fact, Antiochus died suddenly of natural (Daniel would say "divine") causes, either from a fall or from a revolting physical corruption. So his end was as Daniel said.

That Era and Ours

At the conclusion of this chapter Daniel describes his reaction to the vision and the explanation given by the angel Gabriel, saying, "I, Daniel, was exhausted and lay ill for several days. Then I got up and went about the king's business. I was appalled by the vision; it was beyond understanding" (v. 27). When Daniel says that the vision was beyond understanding, we are not to think that he was unable to understand what it foretold would happen, particularly since Gabriel explains it clearly in the second half of the chapter. His confession of failure to understand the vision must refer to his failure to understand why the devastation, destruction, and persecution of his people, which the vision foretold, should be necessary. It is the reason he was appalled. He was appalled in the same way any of us would be if God should give us a vision of some future period of great suffering.

But all this is past, of course—at least if our interpretation is correct. We can see how this affected Daniel. What does it have to do with us? This brings us back to the problems with the second half of Daniel that I raised at the start of this chapter.

Let me suggest two ways we should be affected.

First, predictive prophecy teaches us that the God of the Bible is the true God. This is because the only way that prophecies can come true is if God stands behind them, the true God who alone is able to determine the outcome of history. If the God of the Bible is not the true God, if another, bigger God (or even no God) stands above and behind him, then the God of the Bible cannot control what will happen. Then the prophecies of the Bible, given in his name, will not come to fulfillment. This is not what has happened. These prophecies have come true, and the God of the Bible is thereby shown to be the one true, sovereign God of everything.

Human beings can make shrewd guesses, of course. Soothsayers have done this. The devil can make even shrewder guesses. But history is complex. Human beings are often unpredictable. Therefore, mere guesses, while they are sometimes partially accurate, do not come to fulfillment as the Bible's prophecies do.

Second, predictive prophecy proves that the Bible is the true and trustworthy revelation of this true God. The story of Micaiah is a wonderful illustration of this point. Micaiah lived in the northern kingdom of Israel at a time when Ahab, the king of Israel, wanted to go to war against the king of Aram to capture Ramoth Gilead. He persuaded Jehoshaphat, the king of Judah, to go with him. Jehoshaphat wanted to consult the Lord first. So Ahab called four hundred of the paid court prophets together and asked them, "Shall I go to war against Ramoth Gilead, or shall I refrain?" (1 Kings 22:6).

These men knew who was paying them and what the king of Israel wanted to hear. So they said, "Attack Ramoth Gilead and be victorious . . . for the LORD will give it into the king's hand" (v. 12).

This was more than enough for Ahab. But Jehoshaphat had a little more spiritual sensitivity and was just a bit suspicious of the answer. He said something like, "Look, I don't want to be sticky about this, and I am sure your confidence in these four hundred prophets is well founded. But just to be sure—as a favor to me—isn't there also a prophet of the Lord somewhere from whom we can inquire?"

Ahab's answer is hilarious. I quote it exactly: "There is still one man through whom we can inquire of the LORD, but I hate him because he never prophesies anything good about me, but always bad. He is Micaiah son of Imlah" (v. 8). At this point the two kings had a humorous exchange, but at the end of it Ahab sent for Micaiah.

To get the full force of what happened now, you have to understand something of the geography of Samaria where this took place. Samaria stood on a high ridge of a hill and was surrounded by an enormous wall. In the center of the city was a large square. From that square the one road by which anyone could leave the city passed through the gate and down the ridge to the plain below. This is the road the messenger who was dispatched to get Micaiah would take. So everyone in the armies, the four hundred false prophets, and the two kings who were assembled in the city square could have seen him go. And what is more important, they all would have been watching as Micaiah responded to the king's summons and made his way up that long road, along the ridge, through the gate, and into the city. It was a dramatic scene, a scene right out of one of Cecil B. DeMille's Bible epics.

When the messenger reached Micaiah he warned him to say what the king wanted to hear, and Micaiah responded, "As surely as the LORD lives, I can tell him only what the LORD tells me" (v. 14). But when Micaiah finally stood before the two kings with the eyes of this great priestly and military host upon him, he responded mockingly, saying word for word what the four hundred false prophets had spoken: "Attack and be victorious . . . for the LORD will give it into the king's hand" (v. 15).

Ahab understood that this was not genuine. So he rebuked Micaiah. "How many times must I make you swear to tell me nothing but the truth in the name of the LORD?" he demanded (v. 16).

This time Micaiah spoke in earnest. "I saw all Israel scattered on the hills like sheep without a shepherd, and the LORD said, 'These people have no master. Let each one go home in peace'" (v. 17).

Do you know what Ahab did when he heard that? He turned to Jehoshaphat and said, "Didn't I tell you that he never prophesies anything good about me, but only bad?" (v. 18).

At that point Micaiah went on to additional details, including a specific prediction of Ahab's death. And Ahab did what kings do to unpopular prophets. He threw him in prison and went out anyway to fight against Aram for possession of Ramoth Gilead. Yet before he did this, Micaiah called out, "If you ever return safely, the LORD has not spoken through me" (v. 28). We never hear of Micaiah after that. Perhaps he perished in prison. But we do know what happened to Ahab. He was killed in the battle, and the people were scattered each one to his own town, as Micaiah had prophesied (cf. 1 Kings 22).

The point is obvious. God, the true God, had spoken through Micaiah, his true prophet. And because it was God who had spoken, the word of this God through Micaiah could be trusted.

12

When Shall Messiah Come?

Daniel 9:1–27

Seventy "sevens" are decreed for your people and your holy city to finish transgression, to put an end to sin, to atone for wickedness, to bring in everlasting righteousness, to seal up vision and prophecy and to anoint the most holy.

Know and understand this: From the issuing of the decree to restore and rebuild Jerusalem until the Anointed One, the ruler, comes, there will be seven "sevens," and sixty-two "sevens." It will be rebuilt with streets and a trench, but in times of trouble. After the sixty-two "sevens," the Anointed One will be cut off and will have nothing. The people of the ruler who will come will destroy the city and the sanctuary. The end will come like a flood: War will continue until the end, and desolations have been decreed. He will confirm a covenant with many for one "seven." But in the middle of the "seven" he will put an end to sacrifice and offering. And on a wing of the temple he will set up an abomination that causes desolation, until the end that is decreed is poured out on him.

In the last chapter I began our study of the second half of Daniel with an apology. It was an acknowledgment that Daniel 8–12 is largely prophecy and that this is often difficult to interpret and perhaps at times even more difficult to apply. The section of the book to which we come now is also prophecy. Indeed, it is a decisive passage for all the various systems of prophetic interpretation. I have no apology for this chapter, however, because it is a great chapter. It has two main parts: a prayer of Daniel, which is a model of devout, humble, and effective prayer petition; and a concluding revelation, which was God's answer to that prayer. This concluding prophecy con-

95

cerns the Lord Jesus Christ and is a prediction, not only of the nature of his earthly ministry, but even of the precise time of his appearing and death.

Commentators have called the ninth chapter of Daniel the "key" to prophetic interpretation. Others have called it the "backbone" of prophecy.

Arno C. Gaebelein, a careful scholar who spent much of his life studying and comparing prophetic portions of the Bible, wrote:

> The prophetic message Gabriel brought from the throne of God to Daniel is perhaps the most important not only in the Book of Daniel, but in the whole Bible. The clear understanding of it is indispensable to every reader of God's Word, who wants to know God's purposes concerning the future. In the few verses which contain the words of Gabriel, events relating to Jewish future history are predicted. The return of the Jews from the Babylonian captivity, the rebuilding of the city in time of distress, the coming of Christ in humiliation, his death, the destruction of the temple and the city by the Romans, the desolations and wars which were to follow, all this is prewritten in this great prophecy. The final end of the time of the Gentiles, the great eventful week of seven years is revealed in the last verse.[1]

The Praying Prophet

I have stated that the second half of Daniel is chiefly prophecy as opposed to being chiefly narrative. But it is noteworthy that this, the "backbone" of all prophecies, is nevertheless set in the context of a narrative. At the end of Daniel 8, after Daniel had been given the vision of the ram and goat, we are told that the prophet was troubled by the vision to the point of becoming sick. As we begin Daniel 9, we find what Daniel did to recover from his agitation.

What would you do? In a situation like this I might find myself saying, "Look, James, this business of having visions and then trying to interpret them is pretty tough. It has gotten to the point of actually making you sick, and this means that you have obviously been working too hard. You need a trip, a vacation. You need to get your head together, and then, after you have settled down a bit, you can go at this prophecy business again." Or someone might say, "I think you're losing perspective. What you need is to talk it over with the other court astrologers."

Daniel did not do anything like this. Instead, he did these two things: (1) He studied the Bible, and (2) he prayed. The text says, "In the first year of Darius son of Xerxes . . . I, Daniel, understood from the Scriptures, according to the word of the LORD given to Jeremiah the prophet, that the desolation of Jerusalem would last seventy years. So I turned to the Lord God and pleaded with him in prayer and petition, in fasting, and in sackcloth and ashes" (Dan. 9:1–3). Daniel did not have our Bible. But he had some of it, and he studied what he had. Then, after he knew what the promises of God given in Scripture were, he prayed about them, asking God to do what he had promised.

There are several important points about this. First, Daniel was a prophet himself; nevertheless, he found it important to read the Bible and be instructed by it rather than trusting in some special new revelation. We are not prophets. How much more important a role should Bible study play in our lives!

Second, when Daniel studied the Scripture, God directed him to the passages that spoke most to his need and comforted him by them. Jeremiah had lived in Jerusalem up to the time of its destruction by the Babylonians, and he had predicted that the people would be carried away into captivity and that the captivity would last seventy years. Jeremiah 25 contains the clearest example: "This whole country will become a desolate wasteland, and these nations will serve the king of Babylon seventy years. But when the seventy years are fulfilled, I will punish the king of Babylon and his nation, the land of the Babylonians, for their guilt . . . and will make it desolate forever" (vv. 11–12). Daniel was directed to this passage and concluded from it that the years of captivity were drawing to an end.

It is always difficult to date far-distant events accurately, partly because the ancients did not always reckon time as we do. But in rough terms the dates involved are these. Daniel was probably carried away to Babylon in a partial deportation of the people that took place in 605 B.C., that is, about nineteen years before the city's final destruction in 586 B.C. The vision of this chapter dates from the first year of Darius the Mede, which we can establish from extrabiblical sources as being 538 B.C. This was only forty-eight years after the destruction of the city. But since Jeremiah had spoken of the people *serving* the king of Babylon for seventy years, Daniel probably counted the seventy-year period of captivity from the time of his own deportation; and if that is the case, then sixty-seven years out of the total seventy years had gone by. The termination of the captivity was only three years away. Daniel was over eighty years old at this time. He would not return to Jerusalem. But the assurance that his people would go back and that the city would soon be rebuilt must have been a great comfort to him.

The third thing to notice is that after Daniel had made his discovery, he prayed. Moreover, he prayed for the very thing the Bible had assured him would happen. Does this seem strange to you? There are misguided Calvinists who would conclude in such situations that since God had decreed three more years of captivity and a return to Jerusalem after that, there would therefore be nothing they could do. They could only sit back and let God work. Daniel knew better than that. He knew that although God certainly works according to his own plans and timetable, he nevertheless does this through people—through their acts and attitudes, and particularly their prayers.

Incidentally, Calvin knew better than this too. In his two-volume commentary on Daniel, Calvin has a fifty-page discussion of this prayer (some of the best portions of Calvin's writings are his discussion of prayer, in the

Institutes and elsewhere) in which he insists that knowledge of God's promises stirs us to prayer rather than merely causing us to become detached from God's actions. Calvin says,

> The faithful do not so acquiesce in the promises of God as to grow torpid, and become idle and slothful through the certainty of their persuasion that God will perform his promises, but are rather stimulated to prayer. For the true proof of faith is the assurance when we pray that God will really perform what he has promised us. . . . Nothing . . . can be better for us than to ask for what he has promised.[2]

We do not show our spirituality when we abstain from prayer—"letting God do what God will do"—so much as reveal our carnality. The greatest women and men of God have been prayer warriors.

The Prophet's Prayer

Daniel's prayer is worthy of many studies. It is, as Calvin said, an "example . . . guide . . . [and] kind of common form" for prayer for the whole church.[3] It has three parts. First, it contains a confession of Daniel's and the people's sin (Dan. 9:4–11). Second, there is acknowledgment that it is because of this sin that the just judgments of God had come upon them (vv. 11–14). Third, there is a shift in the prayer to plead for God's mercy (vv. 15–19). These are the three necessary marks of all true prayer: acknowledgment of sin and of the fact that sin always brings judgment and a plea for God's mercy. There is no other way we can approach God except as sinners seeking grace.

Notice one more important thing about this prayer. When Daniel prayed for his people, confessing the sin that caused God to punish them by the deportation, he did not distance himself from his people but rather identified himself intimately with them in his confession. Notice how he uses the first person plural pronoun:

"*We* have sinned and done wrong. *We* have been wicked and have rebelled; *We* have turned away from your commands and laws" (v. 5);

"*we* have not listened to your servants the prophets" (v. 6);

"*we* are covered with shame" (v. 7);

"O Lord, *we* and our kings, our princes and our fathers are covered with shame because *we* have sinned against you" (v. 8);

"*we* have rebelled" (v. 9);

"*we* have not obeyed the Lord our God" (v. 10);

"*we* have sinned against you" (v. 11);

"*we* have not sought the favor of the Lord our God by turning from our sins" (v. 13);

"*we* have not obeyed him" (v. 14);

"*we* have sinned, *we* have done wrong" (v. 15);

"*we* do not make requests of you because we are righteous, but because of your great mercy" (v. 18).

When we confess sin, we have a tendency to confess the sins of other people, or if we do not do that, we confess sin in a manner meant to excuse ourselves. Daniel was not like this. If anyone could have done this, he could have. Nothing bad is said about Daniel in all the Bible. He was only a youth at the time of the fall of Jerusalem, and he had led an exemplary life in the wicked city of Babylon for sixty-seven years. Daniel could have pleaded his innocence. Yet he took the part of his people and confessed his own sin with theirs, saying, "we . . . we . . . we . . . we."

That is the kind of prayer God honors. Daniel prayed with a highly emotional and moving cry, "O Lord, listen! O Lord, forgive! O Lord, hear and act! For your sake, O my God, do not delay, because your city and your people bear your Name." It is no wonder, then, that God sent Gabriel with the revelation with which the chapter ends.

The "Backbone" Prophecy

The revelation God gave Daniel is what I referred to earlier as a "backbone" prophecy, that is, a prophecy that provides a time framework to which most other prophecies can be attached.

> Seventy "sevens" are decreed for your people and your holy city to finish transgression, to put an end to sin, to atone for wickedness, to bring in everlasting righteousness, to seal up vision and prophecy and to anoint the most holy.
>
> Know and understand this: From the issuing of the decree to restore and rebuild Jerusalem until the Anointed One, the ruler, comes, there will be seven "sevens," and sixty-two "sevens." It will be rebuilt with streets and a trench, but in times of trouble. After the sixty-two "sevens," the Anointed One will be cut off and will have nothing. The people of the ruler who will come will destroy the city and the sanctuary. The end will come like a flood: War will continue until the end, and desolations have been decreed. He will confirm a covenant with many for one "seven." But in the middle of the "seven" he will put an end to sacrifice and offering. And on a wing of the temple he will set up an abomination that causes desolation until the end that is decreed is poured out on him.
>
> verses 24–27

This is difficult. But let me take it a step at a time, not presuming to have the only right interpretation—there are many different interpretations—but merely trying to tell you what I think these important paragraphs mean.

First, I am glad to note that the New International Version has done a better job translating this passage than the translators of the King James Version. The King James translators spoke of seventy "weeks," which is unnecessarily misleading, while the more modern translators use the word "sevens." In Hebrew the word actually is the word "seven," or perhaps more accurately "a group of seven" something. It could mean a week because a week is a group of seven days, but it does not actually mean week. And in this case, as nearly all writers recognize, it is a group of seven years. If literal weeks are involved, the prophecy is meaningless, since nothing important occurred within that time framework. If weeks of years are involved, then the time period embraces the years from the giving out of the decree to rebuild Jerusalem to the days of Jesus Christ.

Seventy weeks of years is 490 years, which Gabriel divided into three subperiods: seven weeks of years (that is, 49 years), sixty-two weeks of years (that is, 433 years), and a final period of one week of years (that is, seven years). In one way or another, six things are to be fitted into this period, according to verse 24.

1. Transgression is to be finished.

2. An end is to be made of sin.

3. An atonement for wickedness is to be made.

4. Everlasting righteousness is to be brought in.

5. The vision and prophecy are to be sealed up.

6. The most holy (the Most Holy Place or the most holy One) is to be anointed.

Second, there were a number of decrees having to do with the rebuilding of Jerusalem. Most people recognize that between one of these decrees and the appearance of "the Anointed One" (that is, the Messiah) there should be 483 years, that is, seven plus sixty-two (or sixty-nine) times seven. But because there are different points from which to begin, there are also different ways of arriving at an appropriate year connected to the lifetime of Jesus Christ. There are three main possibilities.

1. The most obvious one from which these 483 years could start is *the decree issued by Cyrus* recorded in 2 Chronicles 36:23 (at the very end of the book) and in Ezra 1:2–4, but this is a number of years too early. Besides, both biblical versions of the decree mention only the reconstruction of the Jerusalem temple. They say nothing about rebuilding the city itself.

2. The second possibility is *the decree issued by Artaxerxes I (464–424 B.C.) in the seventh year of his reign* recorded in Ezra 7:12–26. This decree was issued in 457 B.C. If we move forward forty-nine years from that point, we come to 408 B.C. by which time the walls, streets, and moat around the city were completed. Then moving on 433 more years we come to A.D. 27. (The numbers

bring us to A.D. 26, but it is necessary to add one year to account for the "zero" year when we pass from 1 B.C. to A.D. 1.) This seems a bit early at first. But it is probably just right if we are to understand Gabriel's wording as referring to the start of Christ's ministry. The ministry was•three years long. So this would give us a date for Jesus' death of A.D. 30, which (in my judgment) is exactly right by other calculations.

3. The third possibility is *the decree* recorded by Nehemiah in 2:5–8. This occurred *in the twentieth year of the reign of Artaxerxes I,* which is therefore thirteen years after the earlier decree in Ezra. Calculating from this point brings us to the year A.D. 39 or 40. This seems too late. But it was a popular identification of the time frame years ago, and it was defended by adjusting the years on the basis of a so-called "prophetic year" of 360 days. At one time I was attracted by this possibility, but I now think that the second of these alternatives should be preferred.[4]

By whatever set of calculations one makes, the point is that by the end of the sixty-nine weeks of years the great work of the atonement of the Lord Jesus Christ for sin should be completed.

But what of the last week? What of the final seven years of the 490-year series? This is a puzzle for almost everyone due to the fact that if we simply add seven years to what we have already calculated, we come to the year A.D. 38 (or 46), and nothing of any particular importance happened in that year. At this point Calvin, who has his own system of calculating the earlier years in order to come up to the days of Jesus Christ, departs from strict chronology and regards the final seen years as symbolic of the work of Jesus generally. He regards putting an end to sacrifice in the middle of the "seven" as a way of talking about the resurrection.[5]

Well, it may be so. But I tend to think those people are right who see a break in the fulfillment of prophecy at this point. According to them, the fulfillment of this uniquely Jewish prophecy is suspended while the gospel is preached to the Gentiles and the full number of the church is brought in, a church encompassing people from all walks of life, all races, and all nations. Then after the members of the church are fully gathered, the prophecy will begin to unfold once more with a final week of acute suffering and persecution for the Jewish nation. In this view the last week of Daniel would coincide with a seven-year period of great tribulation mentioned elsewhere. I think there is support for this in Jesus' reference to "the abomination that causes desolation" mentioned in this passage (Dan. 9:27) as well as in Daniel 11:31 and 12:11 as something not to happen immediately, but to be experienced at the very end of the age (Matt. 24:15).

A Word for Today

I end with these conclusions. First, God has a timetable in world history, and he is working carefully according to that plan. This does not mean we are always able to understand his timetable or see his plan. But we know that he is unfolding his timetable and that one day Jesus Christ will come again and all who are in rebellion against him and his kingdom will be judged. Today is a day of God's mercy. But it is not an endless day. The time for turning to Jesus in faith and obedience is limited.

Second, although God works according to his own timetable without deviation, he nevertheless also works through people. That is what we saw when we considered Daniel's prayer of confession, which he prayed in light of God's word that the captivity of the people would last for only three more years. This is another way of saying that what we do for God and in obedience to God counts. We may not see how it counts. When we witness to someone and that person believes in Jesus, we may never see that person again. Or even if we do, we can never know the full extent of what God is accomplishing through our obedience. But we can know that God is doing what he wants to do.

Who knows but that the person we lead to Christ may become the D. L. Moody or the Billy Graham of a future generation?

13

Spiritual Wickedness in High Places

Daniel 10:1-11:1

In the third year of Cyrus king of Persia, a revelation was given to Daniel (who was called Belteshazzar). Its message was true and it concerned a great war. . . .

"Do not be afraid, Daniel. Since the first day that you set your mind to gain understanding and to humble yourself before your God, your words were heard, and I have come in response to them. But the prince of the Persian kingdom resisted me twenty-one days. Then Michael, one of the chief princes, came to help me, because I was detained there with the king of Persia. Now I have come to explain to you what will happen to your people in the future, for the vision concerns a time yet to come."

If you have been studying the Book of Daniel carefully, you may have noticed that the visions of the book tend to increase in length and complexity as they unfold. Or, to put it another way, later visions expand the earlier ones. This feature is particularly evident as we come to the last three chapters. They form a unit, the longest unit in the entire book, and they contain a vision. Up to this point the visions have been handled in one chapter each. Now there is a lengthy vision, presented in chapter 11, to which a preface (chapter 10) and a postscript (chapter 12) are added.

Chapter 10 tells how the vision came to Daniel. Daniel had been mourning for the trials God had shown were to come upon his people, and he had sought assurance from God that they would not be destroyed by the particularly intense persecution that the last part of the preceding vision describes. In fact, he may have been troubled by even more immediate concerns. The third year of the reign of Cyrus in Babylon would have been the year 535/534 B.C., just a few years before Daniel's death.

This places the vision one to two years after the first group of exiles had returned to Jerusalem under Zerubbabel, the Persian-appointed governor of Judah; and Joshua, the high priest. They arrived in the summer of 536 B.C., by autumn had cleared the temple area and resumed the daily sacrifices, and by the following spring had laid the foundation of the temple. But then the work stopped. It stopped for fifteen years until God sent Haggai, one of the minor prophets, to instruct the remnant to resume the work, which they did. By 535/534 B.C. Daniel may have heard of the cessation of the work and been alarmed by it.

The chapter may be studied from a number of directions. It gives insight into Daniel's concern for his people and for the work being done so far away in Jerusalem. It contains important lessons about prayer. Chiefly, however, chapter 10 opens the door on the spiritual warfare that we know from other passages is being waged around the work of God. The chapter begins by saying that the message Daniel received "concerned a great war," described in chapter 11. But before this earthly war is described, we are given a glimpse of a greater earlier war going on in heaven.

War in Heaven

The story recounts how on the twenty-fourth day of the first month of the year (that is, on the twenty-fourth of Nisan, just ten days after the Passover), after Daniel had been mourning and praying for three weeks and as he stood on the bank of the Tigris River, he suddenly saw an angel. Angels are not usually described in much detail in Scripture. But this angel is described as "dressed in linen, with a belt of the finest gold around his waist. His body was like chrysolite, his face like lightning, his eyes like flaming torches, his arms and legs like the gleam of burnished bronze, and his voice like the sound of a multitude" (Dan. 10:5–6). This figure was so overpowering that Daniel's strength fled away and he fell to the ground as if he were in a deep sleep. Even when the angel came to him, touched him, and raised him up, he still stood trembling.

Then the angel spoke. "Do not be afraid, Daniel. Since the first day that you set your mind to gain understanding and to humble yourself before your God, your words were heard, and I have come in response to them. But the prince of the Persian kingdom resisted me twenty-one days. Then Michael, one of the chief princes, came to help me, because I was detained there with the king of Persia. Now I have come to explain to you what will happen to your people in the future, for the vision concerns a time yet to come" (vv. 12–14).

Is that not remarkable? When Daniel prayed, God sent this powerful heavenly being to bring him the vision of the future that we find in chapter 11. But "the prince of the Persian kingdom," whom we must understand to be an evil but correspondingly powerful spirit (not a mere mortal ruler), resisted him so that for three weeks he was not able to come to Daniel. It must have been a great struggle, because it required the special intervention of Michael, the archangel, to resolve it. When Michael was sent, the battle between these good and evil spirits tipped in the direction of the spirit messenger, and he arrived at last to give to Daniel God's message. This is a remarkable glimpse into the battles that are being waged in heaven. Although it is different from anything we find elsewhere in the Word of God, it nevertheless fits what we are taught about spiritual warfare.

The first two chapters of Job are one bit of teaching. These chapters do not speak of outright warfare or struggle, but they show a scene in heaven in which the devil and his angels appear before the throne of God and in which God questions Satan about his righteous servant Job. "Have you considered my servant Job?" God asks. "There is no one on earth like him; he is blameless and upright, a man who fears God and shuns evil" (Job 1:8).

Satan replies that Job fears God only because God has blessed and protected him, and challenges God to take away his possessions, predicting that Job will then curse God to his face. God gives permission. But Job does not curse God. Even after Satan is given permission to take away Job's health, Job does not sin. Instead, he asks, "Shall we accept good from God, and not trouble?" (2:10). He does not charge God with wrongdoing.

In 1 Kings 22 we have another insight into the spiritual warfare that surrounds us and the work God does through his people. This chapter contains the story of Micaiah, a true prophet of the Lord, and the four hundred false prophets of King Ahab. Micaiah told Ahab that he had seen the host of heaven standing around God's throne, suggesting how Ahab might be lured into attacking Ramoth Gilead and meeting his death there. There were a number of suggestions, but finally one spirit said, "I will go out and be a lying spirit in the mouths of all his prophets." That is what happened. Micaiah said, "So now the LORD has put a lying spirit in the mouths of all these prophets of yours. The LORD has decreed disaster for you" (vv. 22–23).

In the next to the last book of the minor prophets there is an even more powerful scene. Zechariah the prophet sees the high priest Joshua (the same one who with Zerubbabel the governor had led the 50,000 Jews back to Jerusalem just a year or two before this vision). He is standing before God's altar, and Satan is there to accuse him. Joshua is clothed in filthy clothes, symbolic of his and the nation's sin, and Satan is no doubt pointing to the filthy garments, asking what right a man so morally deficient has to minister before God in his temple. But God rebukes Satan. And the angel who is accompanying Joshua says to those standing by, "Take off his filthy clothes" (Zech. 3:4). In place of these he is given rich garments and a clean turban, symbolic of the righteousness of God imputed to him (v. 5).

In Revelation 12 there is another scene that has bearing on this warfare. An actual battle is described, involving the same archangel Michael. This text says,

> There was war in heaven. Michael and his angels fought against the dragon, and the dragon and his angels fought back. But he was not strong enough, and they lost their place in heaven. The great dragon was hurled down—that ancient serpent called the devil, or Satan, who leads the whole world astray. He was hurled to the earth, and his angels with him.
>
> Then I heard a loud voice in heaven say:
>
> "Now have come the salvation and the power and the kingdom of our God,
>> and the authority of his Christ.
> For the accuser of our brothers,
>> who accuses them before our God day and night,
>> has been hurled down.
> They overcame him
>> by the blood of the Lamb
>> and by the word of their testimony."
>
> Revelation 12:7–11

This passage is the closest parallel in Scripture to the heavenly messenger's struggle to reach Daniel, recorded in Daniel 10.

The key passage of all these biblical references to spiritual warfare is the concluding portion of Ephesians in which the apostle Paul encourages Christians to arm themselves with God's armor and stand against Satan's power. They are to play their part in these battles.

> Finally, be strong in the Lord and in his mighty power. Put on the full armor of God so that you can take your stand against the devil's schemes. For our struggle is not against flesh and blood, but against the rulers, against the authorities, against the powers of this dark world and against the spiritual forces of evil in the heavenly realms. Therefore put on the full armor of God, so that when the day of evil comes, you may be able to stand your ground, and after you have done everything, to stand. Stand firm then, with the belt of truth buckled around your waist, with the breastplate of righteousness in place, and with your feet fitted with the readiness that comes from the gospel of peace. In addition to all this, take up the shield of faith, with which you can extinguish all the flaming arrows of the evil one. Take the helmet of salvation and the sword of the Spirit, which is the word of God. And pray in the Spirit on all occasions with all kinds of prayers and requests.
>
> Ephesians 6:10–18

According to these verses, the kind of spiritual warfare we see in Daniel affects every Christian.

The Spirit World

We are not told much about the spirit world in the Bible—these passages are only glimpses into the unseen world around us—but we are told what we need to know.

The godly, unfallen angels are mentioned in the Old Testament over one hundred times and in the New Testament more than one hundred sixty times. We are told that they are God's messengers—this is what the word "angel" means. They are immortal; that is, they do not die, though they are created beings and therefore are not eternal. They exist in vast numbers. Revelation speaks of "thousands upon thousands" of them. They possess the elements of personality, for they render intelligent worship to God. Some of these qualities are indicated by the terms used to describe them in Scripture. They are called "the heavenly host" (Luke 2:13). They are called "powers," "dominions," "authorities," and "thrones" (Eph. 1:2; Col. 1:16). In a few cases they are even called gods because they reflect God's glory to us (Ps. 138:1).

Alongside these godly, unfallen angels there is also a vast host of angels who fell with Satan at the time of his original rebellion against God and who are bent on opposing God's rule and doing his people harm. The Bible describes these fallen angels as a terrifying force, not to induce terror in us, but to warn us so that we might draw close to God for protection. The number of this great host can be gauged from the fact that Mary Magdalene alone is said to have been delivered from seven of them (Mark 16:9; Luke 8:2), and from knowing that many, calling themselves Legion, had possessed the man Christ encountered in the territory of the Gerasenes (Luke 8:26–33).

Calvin wrote of God's purpose in telling us of this host:

> We have been forewarned that an enemy relentlessly threatens us, an enemy who is the very embodiment of rash boldness, of military prowess, of crafty wiles, of untiring zeal and haste, of every conceivable weapon and of skill in the science of warfare. We must, then, bend our every effort to this goal: let us not be overwhelmed by carelessness or faintheartedness, but with courage rekindled let us stand our ground in combat.[1]

At the head of these fallen angels is the devil, whom the Bible describes as a powerful foe. There are many jokes about the devil, some possibly inspired by the devil himself to make us think lightly of him and thus lower our guard. But the devil is no lightweight. He is evil, real, and personal.

When we talk about the devil being evil, real, and personal, we must not overexaggerate the case. Because he is a spiritual rather than a material being, many people are inclined to think of Satan more or less as the equal of God. It is true that he is a counterpart of the greatest of the unfallen angels, Michael and Gabriel. But he is not a spiritual counterpart of God. God is

God. Every other being has been created by God and is therefore limited for the simple reason that he or she has been created.

God is omnipotent; he is all-powerful. The devil is not. God can do anything he wishes to do. The devil, like the rest of us, can do only what God permits him to do. This is God's universe, not the devil's. Not even hell is the devil's. God has created hell as the place where he will one day confine Satan and his followers.

God is omnipresent; God is everywhere at once. David said, "Where can I flee from your presence? If I go up to the heavens, you are there; if I make my bed in the depths, you are there. If I rise on the wings of the dawn, if I settle on the far side of the sea, even there your hand will guide me, your right hand will hold me fast" (Ps. 139:7–10).

This cannot be said of Satan. Satan can be in only one place at one time. Consequently, he must either tempt one person in one place at one time, or he must extend his influence through one of the other spiritual beings that fell with him. The result is that, although the devil's influence is widespread, it is probably the case that neither you nor anyone you know has ever been tempted by the devil directly. In fact, in all the Bible we know of only six individuals who were tempted by Satan himself: Eve (but not Adam), Job, Jesus Christ, Judas, Peter, and Ananias (but not his wife Sapphira). No doubt there have been many others, but these are the only ones the Bible tells us of specifically.

God is omniscient; he knows everything. This is untrue of Satan. Satan does not know everything. True, he knows a great deal, and he is undoubtedly a shrewd guesser. But the ways of God must constantly surprise him, and he certainly has no more certainty about what is going to happen in the future than we have.

God's Abiding Truth

Satan is a great and powerful foe, as I have said. Yet we are not to quail before him, but are steadfastly to resist him in the strength and armor of God. Moreover, we are to stand boldly, knowing that, in spite of the opposition of Satan and his hosts, in the final assessment it will be seen that the Word of God and the kingdom of God have prevailed.

I like the way Martin Luther saw it. He was engaged in a great battle himself. The world seemed always to be against him, and behind the terrifying powers of this material world stood the even more terrifying powers of the devil. Luther did not fear. He wrote:

> And though this world, with devils filled,
>   Should threaten to undo us,
> We will not fear, for God hath willed
>   His truth to triumph through us.
> The prince of darkness grim,

We tremble not for him;
His rage we can endure,
For lo! his doom is sure;
    One little word shall fell him.

That Word above all earthly powers,
    No thanks to them abideth;
The Spirit and the gifts are ours
    Through him who with us sideth;
Let goods and kindred go,
This mortal life also;
The body they may kill:
God's truth abideth still;
    His kingdom is forever.

Luther knew that the evil forces of the unseen world are capable of stirring up such hatred against God's saints that we may well lose "goods and kindred" and even our lives. But in this warfare God is still sovereign, and for this reason his "truth" and "his kingdom" will prevail. That is what the angel came to tell Daniel. Daniel saw only the earthly scene (as we do), and his mind was troubled. But God showed that he was in control of history—he showed Daniel how it would all turn out—and Daniel was strengthened by that knowledge. So must we be as we stand for the Lord Jesus Christ, fight on, and look for his coming.

14

The Last Battle

Daniel 11:2–12:4

Those who are wise will instruct many, though for a time they will fall by the sword or be burned or captured or plundered. . . .

At that time Michael, the great prince who protects your people, will arise. There will be a time of distress such as has not happened from the beginning of nations until then. But at that time your people—everyone whose name is found written in the book—will be delivered. Multitudes who sleep in the dust of the earth will awake: some to everlasting life, others to shame and everlasting contempt. Those who are wise will shine like the brightness of the heavens, and those who lead many to righteousness, like the stars for ever and ever.

Several years ago when I first preached through Daniel, one of the elders of Tenth Presbyterian Church told me how much he appreciated the way I was handling the book. "What do you mean?" I asked.

"Well," he said, "instead of going into all the minute details of these prophecies the way some do—and it's not at all certain that they do it accurately—you've tried to extract the main principles and apply them to our lives now."

I said, "Thank you. But I have to warn you that next Sunday evening I come to Daniel 11, and I don't see how I can avoid being specific with that chapter."

He smiled and said, "Well, you're the one who wanted to be an expository preacher."

I suppose that even an expository preacher can find ways to avoid a detailed treatment of a Bible chapter. But it has been clear even up to this point that Daniel does deal with specific points of ancient history; thus, even though the eleventh chapter is difficult, it calls for a detailed explanation. That is what I would like to try to do in this study.

I mention two introductory matters. First, this is the last, longest, most detailed, and therefore most important, prophecy in the book. It has been introduced in chapter 10. It embraces the entire forty-five verses of chapter 11 as well as the first four verses of chapter 12. It concludes with a postscript in 12:5–13. That alone sets it apart as especially significant. Second, the revelation has three parts. That fact helps us to understand the more difficult portions. The first part deals with the history of the Near East from the time of Daniel up to the appearance of Antiochus Epiphanes, whose coming has already been prophesied in earlier chapters. The second part concerns the career of Antiochus himself. Then there is a third part, which is the most difficult. It concerns either Antiochus, the early history of the Roman Empire, or, as I believe, events that are yet to come.

Whatever the difficulties in handling this last part, we are helped in our interpretations by what we are able to decide about the earlier portions of the chapter.

A Detailed History

The first section of chapter 11 extends from verse 1 through verse 19, and concerns the history of the ancient world from the time of Daniel up to the time of Antiochus Epiphanes. It is remarkably detailed. In fact, it is so detailed that John Calvin, who explains each of the references by what was known concerning the history of this period in his time, takes forty pages to spell it out. This is the chief reason the liberal school wants to put the writing of Daniel in the time of the Maccabees, about A.D. 165. It cannot imagine that God can give this kind of detailed information to a prophet many hundreds of years before the events, which is what has happened if the book was written by Daniel during the reigns of Nebuchadnezzar, Belshazzar, Darius, and Cyrus of Persia. That is what the book claims.

The prophecy begins by speaking of three more kings of Persia, and then a fourth who was to be far richer than the others. There is no difficulty in understanding what this means. The rich king is Xerxes, who reigned from 485 to 464 B.C. The kings who preceded him after the death of Cyrus were (1) Cambyses, who reigned from 529 to 523 B.C.; (2) Gaumata, an imposter, who reigned from 523 to 522 B.C.; and finally (3) Darius the Great, who assassinated Gaumata and reigned from 522 to 485 B.C.

The significant thing about Xerxes' reign is that he crossed the Hellespont in an unsuccessful attempt to conquer Europe and was defeated by the Greeks. The Persians had tried to conquer Greece earlier under Darius the Great and had been defeated at Marathon. In this second invasion the great navy of the Persians was defeated by the Greeks at Salamis (in 480 B.C.), and the main body of the Persian army (Herodotus estimated it at a million men) was forced back to Asia. The 100,000-man land army left behind was crushed at the battle of Plataea the following year.

These invasions and attempted subjugation of Greece stuck in the Greek mind and were a major factor in the campaign of Alexander the Great against Persia in the years 334 to 331 B.C., more than a century later. This is what the next verse of Daniel 11 talks about: "Then a mighty king will appear, who will rule with great power and do as he pleases" (v. 3). The next verse shows how the empire of Alexander was to be divided into four parts after his death, which has already been prophesied in the earlier visions.

We have noted this division repeatedly. The significant new item in this verse is the prophecy that not one of the parts of this divided Greek empire would go to even one of Alexander's descendants. That is not what we might have expected; it is not what Alexander himself expected. Nevertheless, it happened. All his descendants, including his wives, children, and even distant relatives, were murdered; and the kingdom was divided into parts eventually ruled by the generals Antipater, Lysimachus, Ptolemy, and Seleucus.

Seleucus ruled over Syria; Ptolemy, over Egypt. From this point on the vision concerns these two kingdoms (the two of the four kingdoms having the most direct bearing on the land and people of Israel).

I do not want to take the time, as Calvin did, to spell out the historical fulfillment of each of the specific prophecies mentioned in verses 5–20. But let me give you one illustration of how accurate and specific these revelations are. In verses 6–9 is a prophecy of a "daughter of the king of the South" who makes an alliance with the "king of the North" but who is unable to retain her place and is handed over together with those who supported her.

This woman's name was Bernice. She was the daughter of Ptolemy II (not the first Ptolemy who assumed the rule of Egypt after Alexander's death), and she married Antiochus Theos of Syria. It was a political marriage. Antiochus had to divorce his first wife to accomplish it. But there were hatred and friction, as one can imagine. Bernice was poisoned, after which Antiochus remarried his first wife. Then Bernice was avenged by her brother, another Ptolemy, who attacked Syria and looted its temples. Josephus, who related this history, records that Ptolemy III returned to Egypt with 4,000 talents of gold, 40,000 talents of silver, and 2,500 objects that had been in the cities and temples of the northern kingdom. This is what verse 8 describes.

Each of the details of this first section of Daniel 11 has had a similarly precise fulfillment in history.

Antiochus Epiphanes

The exceedingly wicked and contemptible king Antiochus Epiphanes has already been mentioned in Daniel, appearing first as "another horn" in the vision of the ram and goat of Daniel 8. In that vision he was identifed as a ruler in the succession of Greek rulers going back to Alexander. Now this wicked ruler appears again (in verses 21–35 of this chapter), and many details about his career are prophesied.

These verses teach that in the early years Antiochus Epiphanes would advance his career by deceit and intrigue, which is what he did. Moreover, they speak of easy victories in these years. The rulers of Egypt had become lax and corrupt, and there were occasions when the king of Egypt did not even attempt to resist Antiochus as he marched through the land. He let him come, and he let him go. Later invasions had a very different outcome, however. On one of these, Antiochus was opposed by the ships and army of the expanding Roman Empire, and he was forced to turn back from Egypt greatly humiliated. What happened then is described in verses 29–33 of this chapter.

It is an interesting story. Antiochus was on his way to invade Egypt again, no doubt expecting the easy victories he had enjoyed earlier. But he was intercepted by the Roman fleet under the command of Popilius Laenas. Popilius was a stern man who demanded that the Greek general return to Palestine. Antiochus said that he would consult his advisors. The Roman knew what Antiochus had in mind. Antiochus wanted time to raise a larger army to repulse the Romans. Instead of granting him time, Popilius with characteristic Roman determination drew a circle in the sand around Antiochus and ordered him to summon his counselors and deliberate on the spot. If he stepped out of that circle without first having agreed to return to Palestine, the Roman officer said he would declare war. Opposed by such determination, Antiochus backed down and went home. But he was furious, as the text in Daniel says he would be.

What is the natural course of human nature when a person is humiliated, as Antiochus was, or forced to back down in a situation over which he or she has no real control? The answer is that generally the person takes his anger out on someone else. This is what Antiochus Epiphanes did. He had been humiliated in front of his army. He could not proceed against Egypt. So he turned against the people of his own territory and poured out his fury there. He led 20,000 men against Jerusalem and abolished the temple worship. Worse, by offering swine's flesh upon it, he desecrated the great altar upon which the daily offerings were made to God. This is "the abomination that causes desolation" of verse 31. As a result of these acts, Antiochus became a symbol of everything the Jewish people most despised and hated, and a widespread, successful rebellion led by Judas Maccabeus was the result.

Presumably "the people who know their God" (v. 32) and "those who are wise" (v. 33) refer to the Maccabees and their followers.

That is the history of the past events prophesied in this chapter, as I see it. And if this is the case—if these prophecies were made when the book claims they were made and if they came true as history shows they came true—then a number of important conclusions follow. First, if the prophecies of this and other biblical books are made in the name of the Bible's God, then this God and not another is the true God. The only way in which these detailed events can be prophesied and then be made to come true is if the true God, the God of the Bible, stands behind them and determines their outcome. No other god can do this, and it proves that this God and not another should be followed.

Second, the fulfillment of prophecies shows that the Bible in which they are recorded is God's book. There are other evidences for the Bible being the Word of God, of course. They are important and, in some cases, sufficient evidences by themselves. But fulfilled prophecy alone, especially detailed prophecy like that in this chapter, validates the Bible as not merely a human document but as God's unique revelation.

Third, the fulfillment of prophecy shows that the God who disclosed these events and then brought them to pass is also able to keep and will keep his promises to his people. When we get in difficult circumstances, our faith sometimes wavers and we wonder whether God is up to our dilemma. We should be encouraged by prophecy to know that nothing is too hard for God. Nothing can ever rise up to thwart his plans. No detail is too small to merit his attention. So if we find Jesus saying, "Surely I am with you always, to the very end of the age" (Matt. 28:20), we can know that he will indeed be with us and that we need not fear circumstances. God is not afraid to make promises to his people because he knows that he can and will keep them. If there were nothing else in this chapter to ponder and take to heart, that alone would be a reason for studying it closely.

The Time of the End

But we still have the final section of this chapter and the verses in Daniel chapter 12 that go with it. These are difficult, as every scholar or commentator acknowledges, and there are many views. Do they relate to history or to events that have not yet occurred? Are they literal or symbolic? The answers to these questions result in quite different approaches, and since there have been great minds arrayed on all sides, it is wise to proceed carefully and with humility.

In my opinion, the fact that there are divergent interpretations is the best evidence for concluding that the events referred to are still future. If the section were referring to past events, there is no reason it should not be as clear in talking about them as the earlier portions of the chapter have been in talking about the history of the ancient Near East from the time of Cyrus to Antiochus Epiphanes. If it were dealing with the past, commentators would agree. If this is the case, then our procedure in studying them must be different. Instead of looking to history to see what happened and then matching those events to the prophecy, we need to study the prophecy itself and see what it seems to be saying about what is yet to come.

Second, I would argue that the verses must be taken as literally as what has gone before. The earlier part of the chapter has spoken of kings and alliances and battles. We have been able to give specific names and dates to these predictions. The same thing should be true for this section, even though we have not yet witnessed the rise or observed the careers of those prophesied. We have no warrant suddenly to substitute a symbolic understanding of the words for a literal one.

Earlier I mentioned that there are three chief approaches to this section. The first is that it is continuing to speak of the career of Antiochus Epiphanes. The best argument for this is that there is no obvious break between verses 35 and 36. So when verse 36 begins, "The king will do as he pleases," it is natural to identify this king as the last-mentioned king of the previous section, Antiochus. The difficulty is that what is said in this section does not fit Antiochus's known career. Calvin in particular notices this, and so do other scholars. It is possible that Antiochus Epiphanes may be a type of a greater evil character prophesied for the last days—I believe that is the case—but if these verses refer to either, it must be the later character and not Antiochus himself whose career is highlighted.

The second view is that these verses prophesy part of the history of the early Roman Empire. This was Calvin's view and he went at it with great thoroughness. No one can easily discount Calvin, of course. But it is significant that Calvin was not entirely satisfied with his own interpretation, at least as I read him. For one thing, he refers to the "king" whose career is described in these verses, not to a specific individual, but to the "kingdom" of the Romans as a whole. He defends this at some length. But if this is right, it is out of step with the way kings are referred to in the first part of the chapter. There "king" refers to a known individual. It should be the same here, in my judgment. Moreover, Calvin has difficulty fixing the details of each prophecy, which is the chief reason I have for saying that the prophesied events must be future.

The third view is that these verses refer to the Antichrist who is said elsewhere to appear at the end of all things—just before the return of Jesus Christ. There are a number of additional reasons for seeing the verses this way. In verse 40 the angel speaks of "the time of the end," which is neither the time of Antiochus Epiphanes or the time of the early Roman Empire. It refers to the end of the world immediately before the final judgment. Since the events of verse 40 are picking up from the verses that have gone before, the phrase "the time of the end" fixes the time frame of this section.

Again, the first verse of chapter 12 begins, "At that time," which means "at the time just described." But what is introduced in chapter 12 is (1) a great persecution, (2) a general resurrection, (3) a final judgment, and (4) the final, eternal blessedness of the saints. The Lord himself took these verses as applying to the last days in his discourse recorded in Matthew 24 and 25. He said, "There will be great distress, unequaled from the beginning of the world until now—and never to be equaled again" (Matt. 24:21). That is not a reference to the Maccabees but to the time of persecution immediately preceding his return.

At this point I want to be particularly cautious. But if what I have said thus far is correct, then it would seem best to regard these verses as a prophecy of the career of the Antichrist and of the final great battle of Armageddon that is described elsewhere in Scripture. I think in particular of Ezekiel 38 and of Revelation 16 and 19. How we handle Daniel 11:36–12:4 will depend in some measure, then, on what we think of the chapters in Ezekiel and Revelation. But taking them together, I find that they refer to a great world war immediately prior to the Lord's return. Daniel refers to a great battle between the kings of the North and the South. He mentions Egypt particularly as well as Libya and Nubia. Ezekiel also mentions a group of southern nations, and he speaks of a great northern power in terms that made me think of Russia.[1] These engage in a war, which in Revelation is called Armageddon.

At the end of this period of great international turmoil, the Lord Jesus Christ returns, subdues his and our enemies, and ushers in a kingdom that shall never be overturned or destroyed. If this is the way these verses are to be taken, then they deal with the same events prophesied at the conclusion of the dream given to Daniel as recorded in chapter 7. There the Antichrist is overthrown, and all "authority, glory and sovereign power" are given to the Son of Man. The text says, "His dominion is an everlasting dominion that will not pass away, and his kingdom is one that will never be destroyed" (Dan. 7:14).

"What Shall the Righteous Do?"

I realize that the interpretation of Daniel 11:36–12:4 that I have given here may be wrong and that some will disagree with it. But in a sense, it does not matter a great deal who these factions are or how this great final battle will turn out—if there is a final battle. I say that because in one sense all we have here is a description of an intensifying of that distress and persecution that Christians have known in all ages and that they have been called upon to endure for the sake of their love for and commitment to Jesus Christ. Even Calvin approaches the passage like this at one point, saying that the church is to be "subject to most numerous and grievous calamities until the advent of Christ, but yet it should feel God's propitious disposition, enduring its own safety under his aid and protection."[2]

The bearing of these things on our lives is that we are to live for the Lord Jesus Christ and honor him regardless of the circumstances.

Years ago someone preached a sermon on Psalm 11:3, which asks the probing question: "When the foundations are being destroyed, what can the righteous do?" The preacher asked the question and then answered, "Why, go on being righteous, of course." That is what Daniel is saying in the middle of this chapter in one of my favorite Bible verses, though I prefer it in the King James Version. "The people who know their God will firmly resist him" (Dan. 11:32). Or as the King James Version has it, "The people that do know their God shall be strong, and do exploits." Daniel is saying that there is always going to be wickedness in this world. There will always be wars and rumors of wars, famine, trouble, persecutions, and distress. He had them in his day. We have them in ours, and they will be present even at the end of this age. Nevertheless, those who know God are to stand firm, live righteous lives, resist evil, and do exploits, as God prospers them.

15

Until the End Comes

Daniel 12:5–13

Then I, Daniel, looked, and there before me stood two others, one on this bank of the river and one on the opposite bank. One of them said to the man clothed in linen, who was above the waters of the river, "How long will it be before these astonishing things are fulfilled?"

The man clothed in linen, who was above the waters of the river, lifted his right hand and his left hand toward heaven, and I heard him swear by him who lives forever, saying, "It will be for a time, times and half a time. When the power of the holy people has been finally broken, all these things will be completed."

I heard, but I did not understand. So I asked, "My lord, what will the outcome of all this be?"

He replied, "Go your way, Daniel, because the words are closed up and sealed until the time of the end. Many will be purified, made spotless and refined, but the wicked will continue to be wicked. None of the wicked will understand, but those who are wise will understand.

"From the time that the daily sacrifice is abolished and the abomination that causes desolation is set up, there will be 1,290 days. Blessed is the one who waits for and reaches the end of the 1,335 days.

"As for you, go your way till the end. You will rest, and then at the end of the days you will rise to receive your allotted inheritance."

At a first reading, the last nine verses of Daniel are a letdown. They are a postscript to the final, great vision of 11:2–12:4, which is long, detailed, and comprehensive. That section traces the history of the world from the age of Daniel under the kings of Persia through the age of the Greeks up to the time of the persecutions under Antiochus Epiphanes. Then it skips ahead (according to my understanding) to the time of great persecution at the end of history and the end of that age by a general resurrection of all persons and the final judgment. By contrast, in the postscript we find Daniel seeking understanding of things that are beyond him.

It is worse than that. The section begins with a description of two angels in addition to the one who brought the revelation to Daniel. And *they* are confused. In the New Testament, in 1 Peter 1:12, the apostle speaks of Old Testament teachings that were puzzles even to the angels. Here we have an example, as one of the angels asks, "How long will it be before these astonishing things are fulfilled?" (Dan. 12:6). The angel did not know the time of these events, and neither do we. In fact, even after the first angel gave the answer, "It will be for a time, times and half a time" (v. 7), Daniel still did not understand (v. 8), and the angel did not really enlighten him. The angel's final words confuse the matter even further. For he ends by speaking of a period of 1,290 days and another of 1,335 days, and to my knowledge no one has ever conclusively shown what those two periods refer to.

Yet this postscript to the vision of 11:2–12:4 is not without value. For it gives a description of the characteristics of the last days and tells how the righteous are to live in them. We may not be living in the very last days now. The Lord may not return for centuries. But every age has characteristics of the last days, and believers are always to live as Daniel was to live, until the end comes.

Knowledge without Understanding

In this last chapter of Daniel there is emphasis on understanding—a lack of understanding by the wicked and a desire for understanding by the righteous. But to see what is involved it is necessary to go back to the closing sentence of verse 4, which says, "Many will go here and there to increase knowledge." Going "here and there" is a Hebrew idiom suggesting a frantic but futile pursuit of something illusive (cf. Amos 8:11–12). So the idea is that in the last days people will embark on a pursuit of knowledge, thinking that it will lead to understanding, but they will not find it.

There are few things more characteristic of our age than this. At no time in the history of the world have more things been known by more people. Education is a major industry. Yet at no time have people seemed more to lack understanding. Millions do not even know who they are, let alone why they are or what they are doing.

We have a crisis in the area of learning today, which I explain as a failure of the two main approaches to knowledge. The first approach is to seek knowledge *by reason alone*. It goes back to the Greeks, particularly to Plato, who taught that knowledge is not in the mere observation of things but in perceiving their eternal and unchangeable essence. He expressed this as a study of forms or ideals rather than particulars. Our form of this approach is modern science, which seeks for laws or principles through what we call the scientific method.

This method is not all bad because it has given us the kind of technical progress we have known in the developed world since the Industrial Revolution. But this approach does not have all the answers either. On the contrary, it has great weaknesses. One of these is the way it tends to treat all things impersonally, including persons. If reality is ultimately a scientific equation, then people are basically only rather complex machines—and can be treated as such. There are some who are saying this. Communism reduces reality to economic forces and has no difficulty manipulating people, even killing them, for its ends. The renowned Harvard professor B. F. Skinner is another example. He believes in the scientific "conditioning" of people for the "good" of society.

An approach to knowledge by reason alone is not adequate for ethics. It tells what can be done, but it does not tell what ought to be done. As a result of these weaknesses, within recent memory we have seen a whole generation revolt from this approach to learning.

The other approach to understanding is *by the senses* or emotional experience. It says, "If you can't get to reality by reason, try feelings. If the mind is inadequate, try the heart." People have. They have tried to get in touch with the universe or just with themselves by sexual experimentation, drugs, encounter sessions, psychiatry, and a revival of Eastern mystical religions.

Is this valid? Up to a point the desire to discover or express one's feelings is valid, because we are emotional beings. That is, we have hearts as well as heads. We need to feel. We need close emotional and physical relationships. But important as this is, it cannot be the basis for true understanding simply because it is not lasting. Emotional "highs" are always followed by emotional "lows." Experience fluctuates. Besides, mere emotion does not satisfy the mind. The chief example here is the drug culture, which for a time was put forward as the way to get in touch with reality. People who have been under the influence of drugs would speak of perceiving things never perceived before. But when asked, "What exactly did you perceive? What did you learn by the experience?" they are unable to give reasonable answers.

So there really is something like a crisis in the field of learning, and many people are asking if there is not another way. The Christian replies that there is indeed another way based on the fact that reality is neither an equation nor an emotional experience. It is found in the God of the Bible who is the author of but who transcends both emotion and reason. Therefore, to know him is to have knowledge. Wise old Solomon said, "The fear of the LORD is the beginning of wisdom, and knowledge of the Holy One is understanding" (Prov. 9:10).

Moreover, this approach is strong at precisely those points where the other steps toward knowledge are weak. This is so because of who God is. The rationalistic approach is weak because it makes reality impersonal. But God is a personal being. He loves and cares for us. He reveals himself by name. He enters our history as the Lord Jesus Christ to draw us to himself. The rationalistic approach is weak also because it fails to give an adequate base for ethics. But the God of the Bible is the ethical God. "Right" flows from his character. When we turn to the other approach to knowledge, the approach through emotional experience, and note its weaknesses—the fact that it is passing and does not last, and that it fails to satisfy the mind—the answer is again in the nature of the Bible's God. God is eternal and unchangeable, the same yesterday and today and forever, and he reveals himself to our minds propositionally in the pages of his written Word.

The world does not have this approach to knowledge; therefore, its experience is what the angel predicted in his words to Daniel: a frantic pursuit of knowledge without true understanding. It is because the key to knowledge is lacking.

An Increase of Wickedness

The second characteristic of the last days, suggested by reference to a final judgment in verse 2 but explicitly spelled out in verse 10, is an increase in wickedness. Verse 10 says of the saints, "Many will be purified, made spotless and refined," but it adds of those who are not God's people, "the wicked will continue to be wicked." Indeed, they will break the power of God's people in some great final catastrophe (v. 7), the most wicked among them having ushered in the period of intense suffering and persecution in which the abomination that causes desolation is set up (v. 11).

I do not think we are in this period of final intense persecution today, but we do live in wicked times. Paul wrote to Timothy of the last days, saying, "There will be terrible times in the last days. People will be lovers of themselves, lovers of money, boastful, proud, abusive, disobedient to their parents, ungrateful, unholy, without love, unforgiving, slanderous, without self-control, brutal, not lovers of the good, treacherous, rash, conceited, lovers of pleasure rather than lovers of God—having a form of godliness but denying its power" (2 Tim. 3:1–5).

What a horrible picture! We tend to read it and turn away exclaiming, "Spare us such days!" But those verses are actually descriptive of our days, although we give other names to the vices Paul mentions. "Lovers of themselves" we call narcissism. "Lovers of money" is materialism. "Boastful, proud, abusive" is "letting it all hang out." We call "disobedient to parents" the generation gap. And so on with all the other failures of our age.

Therefore, I repeat: I do not think we are yet living in this particularly wicked age of final persecution before the Lord comes. *But we are living in something quite like it.* And we can hardly be surprised if the evil we see now intensifies and the persecutions we witness increase dramatically in the years to come.

The first chapter of Romans explains why and how this happens. It shows that the only way in which a civilization moves upward from barbarism is by a genuine and growing knowledge of God. It is what I said earlier when I quoted from Proverbs: "The fear of the LORD is the beginning of wisdom, and knowledge of the Holy One is understanding." That is the way a people, nation, or culture advances. But what happens if knowledge of God is neglected or spurned, as Paul says the wicked do spurn it? In that case, people are cut off from what is good and enter upon a downhill course that results in their increasing spiritual, moral, and physical debasement. In each instance, Paul uses the phrase "God gave them over," and shows the result of rejecting knowledge of the true God. First, they are given over to "sexual impurity" (v. 24). Second, they are given over to "shameful lusts" (v. 26). Third, they are given over to "a depraved mind," in which they justify their evil deeds by calling good evil and evil good (vv. 28–32).

That is precisely the point to which our culture has come today. We have been given over to sexual impurity, to shameful lusts, and to a depraved mind. Indeed, few things are so characteristic of our time as the use of words to justify evil and disparage the good. Vices that in an earlier time would have been considered abhorrent are now justified as "self-expression," "personal growth," "an alternative lifestyle," "freedom of choice," "honesty," or similar "good" things.

It is not impossible that a time like ours could lead rapidly into the final period of intense persecutions described by the angel: "a time, times and half a time" (presumably a period of three and half years, cf. 7:25) or the special period of 1,290 or 1,335 days (which we cannot yet explain), referred to at the end of this chapter.

The Way of the Righteous

The point of this chapter is not to describe the wickedness of the final days, however. That has already been adequately described in the preceding visions. Nor is it even to describe the wickedness of Daniel's own day (or ours). The evil of his age was vividly known to Daniel already. No, the point of the chapter is to encourage God's people to triumph in the midst of evil. How are they to do that? This last section of Daniel suggests two things.

First, the people of God are to live by faith in God and by the knowledge of God given in his written revelation. This is the point of the angel's words to Daniel regarding the scroll on which this book was written. The angel said, "Go your way, Daniel, because the words are closed up and sealed until the time of the end" (Dan. 12:9). Sometimes this verse is understood as if it were teaching that the book was to be withdrawn from circulation until the time of the end when it would have its seal broken and would again be read and understood. But that is hardly right, since the book has been known and read (though not always fully understood) from Daniel's time until our own. I think Gleason Archer is right when he sees the words implying official validation of the book as a true revelation from God. He writes, "The words of prophecy [are] 'closed up' . . . as an official, validated document. The words are also to be 'sealed' . . . by the recording scribe, Daniel himself, as a faithful transcript of God's revealed truth."[1] In other words, this was the trustworthy, validated revelation according to which Daniel was to live in those days.

But even if this refers to the sealing up of prophecies not yet understood until a later time when they will be understood, we can hardly fail to compare this last chapter of Daniel with the last chapter of Revelation. The latter is the closest parallel in the New Testament to Daniel 12. In Daniel the prophet is told to "close up" and "seal" the prophecy. But in Revelation the angel tells the apostle John, "Do not seal up the words of the prophecy of this book, because the time is near. Let him who does wrong continue to do wrong; let him who is vile continue to be vile; let him who does right continue to do right; and let him who is holy continue to be holy" (Rev. 22:10–11).We live after the days of the apostle John. So even if the words of Daniel's prophecy were sealed up because the people of that time could not understand them, we are no longer living in such times and the entire Word of God is open for us to read and understand.

This does not mean that God has revealed all his secrets to us. There is much we have not been told. Deuteronomy speaks of these things, saying, "The secret things belong to the LORD our God." That is, they are God's business, not ours. But that same verse goes on to say, "But the things revealed belong to us and to our children forever, that we may follow all the words of this law" (Deut. 29:29). That is the point, you see. There is much we do not know. There will always be much about God we will not know. But God has revealed what we need to know, and we are to treasure these revealed truths and live by them.

To live by faith in God and by the knowledge of God given in his written revelation is the first secret to living for God in the last days.

Second, the angel spoke to Daniel about the righteous being "purified, made spotless and refined" (Dan. 12:10). Or to go back to the concluding words of the vision of 11:2–12:4, "Those who are wise will shine like the brightness of the heavens, and those who lead many to righteousness, like the stars for ever and ever" (Dan. 12:3). This combination of ideas—purification, refinement, spotless living, and shining with the brightness of the heavens—speaks of the actual personal righteousness of God's elect people, which by the blessing of God inevitably leads others to believe in God and become like God themselves. It is what we are called upon to be and do as the end approaches.

Whenever the Bible speaks of the people of God shining like the stars (or whatever), it is speaking of their showing forth the character of God by their own acts of righteousness as a result of spending time with him. After Moses had spent time with God on the mountain, his face shone with a transferred brilliance—so much so that the people asked that he cover his face with a veil until the glory of God visible in his face should subside (Exod. 34:29–35; 2 Cor. 3:7–18). Moses revealed God's glory as a result of having spent time with him, and this is what Paul picks up in 2 Corinthians to argue that we also are to reflect God's glory to others.

We do not always do it well. We are like the moon. When the sun goes down and the moon comes up, the moon shines. But it does not shine by its own light. It shines only by reflecting light from the sun. Sometimes it is a full moon, and the sky is filled with light. At other times it is a new moon, barely visible. Or else it is a tiny quarter, and we cannot tell whether it is a waxing or a waning quarter. Our job is to reflect the light of God's glory so that people living in our own dark age might see the light and be drawn to its true source.

Those who shine with God's glory will lead many to righteousness, as the angel told Daniel they would.

Finally, in the very last verse of the book Daniel is told to "go [his] way till the end," knowing that he would eventually rest and receive his inheritance at the end of days. It was a way of telling him that, though the days ahead would be bad, his task was to persevere and not waver in his stand for God. So also with us. Is that what you are doing in this age? Are you wise in spiritual things because you have filled your mind with God's written revelation? Do you spend time with God? And because you have spent time with God, do you reflect his character to our darkened world? Do you lead others to Christ? Are you God's witness? This is what God has given us to do. It is our commission and task and opportunity.

Notes

Chapter 1: *Whose God Is God?*

1. Arthur Jeffery, "Introduction to the Book of Daniel," in *The Interpreter's Bible*, vol. 6, ed. George Arthur Buttrick (New York and Nashville: Abingdon, 1956), 345.

2. James A. Montgomery, *A Critical and Exegetical Commentary on the Book of Daniel*, the International Critical Commentary series (Edinburgh: T. & T. Clark, 1927), 1ff.

3. Cited by Montgomery, *A Critical and Exegetical Commentary on the Book of Daniel*, 57–58.

4. Gleason L. Archer, "Daniel," in *The Expositor's Bible Commentary*, vol. 7, ed. Frank E. Gaebelein (Grand Rapids: Zondervan, 1985), 8.

5. Augustine, *The City of God*, in *A Select Library of the Nicene and Post-Nicene Fathers of the Christian Church*, vol. 2, ed. Philip Schaff (Grand Rapids: Eerdmans, 1977), 282–83.

6. See Philip Edgcumbe Hughes, *Christianity and the Problems of Origins* (Philadelphia: Presbyterian and Reformed, 1974), 11.

7. Portions of the material on the two cities are adapted from a longer discussion in my book *Foundations of the Christian Faith* (Downers Grove, Ill.: InterVarsity, 1986), 664–68.

Chapter 2: *A Young Man Decides*

1. John Calvin, "Dedicatory Epistle," in *Commentaries on the Book of the Prophet Daniel* (Grand Rapids: Eerdmans, 1948), lxiv–lxv. The historical data are from an introduction by Wilbur M. Smith.

2. J. C. Ryle, *Holiness: Its Nature, Hindrances, Difficulties and Roots* (Cambridge: James Clarke, 1959), 41.

3. Ryle's eight points are found on pages 40–44.

Chapter 3: *God of the Nations*

1. John Calvin, *Commentaries on the Book of the Prophet Daniel* (Grand Rapids: Eerdmans, 1948), 141.

2. A. W. Tozer, *The Knowledge of the Holy* (New York: Harper & Row, 1961), 66–67.

Chapter 4: *Rock of Ages*

1. I deal with this argument for inspiration from other texts in my book *Standing on the Rock* (Wheaton, Ill.: Tyndale House, 1984), 59–60.

2. So much has been written on both sides of this question that it is not possible to list adequate references here. For a more extensive treatment, see my book *The Last and Future World* (Grand Rapids: Zondervan, 1974).

Chapter 7: *Belshazzar Gave a Party*

1. Ferdinand Hitzig, *Das Buch Daniel* (Leipzig: Weidman, 1850), 75.

2. Alan Millard, "Daniel and Belshazzar in History," *Biblical Archeology Review* (May-June 1985): 75–77.

Chapter 8: *A Busy Man's Devotional Life*

1. Gleason L. Archer, *Encyclopedia of Bible Difficulties* (Grand Rapids: Zondervan, 1982), 287.

2. These and other comments are recorded by Franky Schaeffer in *A Time for Anger: The Myth of Neutrality* (Westchester, Ill.: Crossway Books, 1982), 28–33.

Chapter 9: *History by the Ounce*

1. In order to avoid truly predictive prophecy, the liberal school dates the writing of Daniel about 165 B.C. and views the four kingdoms as (1) the Babylonian kingdom, (2) the kingdom of the Medes, (3) the kingdom of the Persians, and (4) the Greek Empire—all of which would therefore have come on the stage of history by the time of the book's writing. See the preceding chapter.

2. See Gleason L. Archer, "Daniel," in *The Expositor's Bible Commentary,* vol. 7 (Grand Rapids: Zondervan, 1985), 86.

Chapter 10: *A Vision of Jesus Christ*

1. S. Mowinckel, *He That Cometh,* trans. G. W. Anderson (New York: Abingdon, 1954).

Chapter 11: *End of an Era*

1. Gleason L. Archer, "Daniel," in *The Expositor's Bible Commentary,* vol. 7 (Grand Rapids: Zondervan, 1985), 103.

Chapter 12: *When Shall Messiah Come?*

1. A. C. Gaebelein, *The Prophet Daniel: A Key to the Visions and Prophecies* (New York: Publication Office "Our Hope," n.d.), 129–30.

2. John Calvin, *Commentaries on the Book of the Prophet Daniel,* vol. 2 (Grand Rapids: Eerdmans, 1948), 135–36.

3. Ibid., 185.

4. For a balanced discussion of the three views, see Gleason L. Archer, "Daniel," in *The Expositor's Bible Commentary,* vol. 7 (Grand Rapids: Zondervan, 1958), 113–16.

5. John Calvin, *Commentaries on the Book of the Prophet Daniel,* 2:226.

Chapter 13: *Spiritual Wickedness in High Places*

1. John Calvin, *Institutes of the Christian Religion,* ed. John T. McNeill and trans. Ford Lewis Battles, vol. 1 (Philadelphia: Westminster Press, 1960), 173.

Chapter 14: *The Last Battle*

1. See my book *The Last and Future World* (Grand Rapids: Zondervan, 1964), 105–7. Meshech and Tubal correspond to the two great halves of the modern state of Russia: Moscow and Tobolsk. Moscow is on the Moskva River; Tobolsk is on the Tobol. Besides, the Hebrew word for "chief prince" in Ezekiel 38:2 is *rosh,* which could be the popular noun from which we get the word "Russian." The great Hebrew lexicographer Gesenius thought so, for he noted that the Byzantine writers of the tenth century referred to the Russians as *hoi Rhōs.*

2. John Calvin, *Commentaries on the Book of the Prophet Daniel,* vol. 2 (Grand Rapids: Eerdmans, 1948), 368.

Chapter 15: *Until the End Comes*

1. Gleason L. Archer, "Daniel," in *The Expositor's Bible Commentary,* vol. 7 (Grand Rapids: Zondervan, 1985), 156.

Subject Index

Scripture Index

Genesis
1:26—82
10:8–12—34
11:1–9—34
11:7—82
18:1—82
18:17—82
41:16—30
41:25—30
41:40—60
41:44—60

Exodus
20:3–6—45
34:29–35—124

Deuteronomy
18:15—85
18:18—85
29:29—123

2 Samuel
7:19—83

1 Kings
Chap. 22—93–94, 105
22:6—93–94

2 Chronicles
36:23—100

Ezra
1:2–4—100
7:12–26—100

Nehemiah
2:5–8—101

Job
1:8—105
2:10—105

Psalms
Ps. 2—40
8:4–5—54
11:3—116
110:1—83
118:22—37
138:1—107
139:7–10—108

Proverbs
9:10—120

Isaiah
6:1—82
8:14—38
Chap. 14—51
14:13–14—51
28:16—38
41:21–24—36

Jeremiah
Chap. 25—97

Ezekiel
Chap. 28—55
Chap. 38—116

Daniel
Chap. 1—21, 90
Chaps. 1–6—15
Chaps. 1–7—90
1:1–2—13–18
1:3–21—19–25
1:8—21

133